"Fired a Gun at the Rising of the Sun": The Diary of Noah Robinson of Attleborough in the Revolutionary War

Transcribed and Annotated by
Robert A. Geake

Forward

Noah Robinson was born in the town of Attleborough, Massachusetts on March 22, 1758. He was the first son of Zepheniah Robinson and Deborah Stanley Robinson. His brother Philip would be born November 20, 1760[1]. Noah was named for his Grandfather, Lt. Noah Robinson (1702-1788). With the outbreak of the Revolutionary War, Robinson enlisted on April 21, 1777 in Captain Stephen Richardson's company which marched to Rhode Island that date "to hold the Lines until men could be raised for that purpose". His company remained for two months. He served another 52 days as private in Capt.ain Israel Trow's from May 14, 1777 through July 6th.. In September, he enlisted with Colonel Danforth Keye's regiment, serving as a private in Rhode Island from September 1, 1777 until January 1, 1778. He would later serve in Captain Moses Wilmarth's company of Colonel John Daggett's regiment, 2 months and 18 days in Rhode Island from January through March 1778. Robinson served as Sergeant the following year in Capt. Enoch Richardson's company from August 12, 1779 through September 11, 1779[2]. He was well educated, and performed duties as clerk or scribe for each of the captains under whom he served[3]. His journal describes the daily routine of many militias as well as his company's involvement in the Rhode Island campaign[4].

---

[1] Carter, Marion Pearce *Baptizms, Marriages, Deaths, Admitted to Communion Old Town Church, Attleboro. First Church 1740-1856* Attleboro, 1928 Vol. VI, pp. 5, 6

[2] (*Massachuseets Soldiers and Sailors of the American Revolution*, Boston, Wright & Potter, 1905 Vol. 13, p. 460

[3] Karen Eberhart, Researcher's Guide for the Noah Robinson Diaries, RIHS MSS 1132 Historical note 1

[4] *Diaries of Noah Robinson*, MSS 1132, five volumes, 1777-1781, Collection of Men's Diaries. Robinson Research Library, Rhode Island

Of equal importance, his journal records life in a militia encampment with its drudgery of daily duties, the endless search for provisions, and the parading for exercise that strived to keep the men in some semblance of military readiness.

Rumors, news of far away battles, and discord within the encampments are also detailed, as well as his family, neighbors, fellow soldiers, and the social life of his home town of Attleboro during the years of the war.

Robinson exhibited artistic talent within his journal as well. The days and dates on these pages are often flourished with an elegant style of penmanship, and "draughings" with similarities to the primitive, but detailed American style that found its way into other journals, as well as whalehorn, chests, and eventually wood and canvas in the early years of the Republic.

Of note, especially as he was employed as a scribe for the regimental officers, are the spelling errors, lack of punctuation, undotted "I's" and uncrossed "T's" as well as run on sentances throughout the journal, may be ascribed to Robinson's habit of composing his entries at the close of day, when he was often "on the flower" or both tired and exhillerated from hours of conversation, or sexual activity. These dalliances, while sometimes written of in a boastful manner, were also at times disguised by use of a single initial to name the woman, or the initials of the person's name flourished by his pen into an indecipherable symbol. Other more common alliances were written in the former manner and seldom name any individual among "the ladies" that visited the Officers Quarters. These dalliances however, were often underscored by later written entreaties to "His Most Omnipotent" that he might "learn thy will".

Noah Robinson would marry Abigail Draper(1760-1836) on 28 March 1782, and they would have two children, Nabbie R. Robinson (1783-1836) and a son named Noah, born 18 September 1785, who would live less than a year.

Gravestones of Noah Robinson and his infant son, First Congregational Church, Falls Cemetery,   North Attleboro MA.. Photo by Robert A. Geake

Noah Robinson died 30 June 1788.

Vol. 1. Noah Robinson's Journal Being in the Service of the N. England States in Capt. Caleb Richardson's Company[5], Col. Keyes[6] Regt. D 1777

[5] Caleb Richardson served as Captain in Col. Timothy Walker's regiment, and commanded the men raised in Attleboro and Easton for Col. Daggett's regiment. Noah Robinson first served in Capt. Stephen Richardson's company, which was comprised of roughly one-quarter of the militia from Attleboro. He was among those men sent into Rhode Island in April 1777 to "hold the lines until men could be raised for that purpose". It is unknown whether he recorded his first months of service ending on May 15, 1777. It is also unclear whether he continued to serve throughout that summer, or if he re-enlisted at the time this journal begins and he is again with Captain Caleb Richardson. (*Massachuseets Soldiers and Sailors of the American Revolution*, Boston, Wright & Potter, 1905 Vol. 13, p. 230)

[6] Colonel Danforth Keyes was among those minutemen from Brookfield, Massachusetts who "answered the alarm' In April 1775, and by May 19th was Lt. Col. in a company of men camped in Roxbury, second in command to Colonel Ebenezer Learned. His was one of nine companies comprising of 465 men, posted in Roxbury, Dorchester, and Watertown by June 15, 1775. (MSSRW, Vol. 9, pp 150-151)

September 23rd (1777)
This morning about 9 o'clock Marched from home to
Bradforts from thence to Pawtuxett[7] and Dined the Rainey
Day.
Wednesday 24th
This morning cloudy & wet However Marched off to Warwick
Mills[8] to Breakfast then to North Ferry and took Barraks.
Thursday 25th
Nothing Strange- However I went on guard at Night and
Rainey it was Come of in the morning.
Friday 26th
I went to Ol New Town and Drawd Rum for the Guard last
Night it being Rainey.
Saturday 27th
Nothing Strange to Day. Built us a Bunk to Lodge[9].
Sunday 28th
In the forenoon went after Grapes. Afternoon was at Capt.
Richardsons quart(ers). Nothing Remarkable.
Monday 29th

---

[7]The village name was adapted from the indigenous language, meaning
"Little Falls" for the small waterfall where the Pawtuxet River empties into
the harbor and Narragansett Bay. Namquid Point (now Gaspee) a long
sandbar that lies below this harbor the H.M.S. Gaspee, a British patrol ship
chasing smugglers, ran aground and was attacked and burned by men
from Providence and Pawtuxet on the night of June 9, 1772. At the time of
the Revolution, it was a flourishing maritime town.

[8] Warwick, Rhode Island historian Henry A.L. Brown believes Robinson
refers to an area where some of the first mills were established along what
is now Old Mill Creek as it empties into the cove below Conimicut Point.

[9] Shelter made by soldiers were often crude log-cabin like structures
whose inner bunks would have been planks nailed upon posts for support,
usually in a "bunk" style manner around the interior walls, and a wood
stove in its center.

Orders to Clean our Arms today. Drawd Louance today. Company Paraided at night and was viewed by Lt. Fullor. I Went on guard at Night.

Tuesday 30th
Dismissed the guard So we choose a (?) in the (?). Afternoon walked around our encampment.
Wednesday, October 1st 1777
Last night about 12 oc'clock was turned out by our sentinels Firing but for no purpose. Pleasant morning so I awoke and plunged my Self in to the Sea. I sent my clothes to be washed. Orders to be ready to March at the Shortistt Notis-Afternoon walked about one mile with Sgt. Tiff[10].
Thursday 2nd
Awoke and went after Provisions in Afternoon Lt. James come in with five men.
Friday 3rd
In the forenoon Playd quaits[11] with the officers (,) the afternoon Drank Cyder.
Saturday 4th
In the forenoon Paraided for Exercise[12]. Nothing Strange today.

---

[10] Noah Tiffany enlisted on May 1, 1775. He served in Capt. Stephen Richardson's company of militiamen, and later that year in Capt. Caleb Richardson's Company of Walker's regiment and received a coat while encamped in Roxbury into November. He served another five months in 1776, and was among the men with Robinson, sent into Rhode Island in the effort of April 1777 to "hold the line" for reinforcements. (MSSRW Vol. 15, p. 738)

[11] The colonial version of ring-toss or horseshoes.

[12] When "Parading for Exercise", a company was to be formed "in two ranks at one pace distance, with the tallest man in the rear, and both ranks fixed with the shortest man of each in the centre. A Company thus drawn up is to be divided into two factions or platoons; the Captain to take posit on the right of the left platoon, also covered by a Sergeant; the Ensign four paces behind the centre of the Company; the First Sergeant two paces behind the second platoon; the other two Corporals are to be the flank of

Sunday 5th
Paraided for Exercise Afternoon and had our Arms viewed by
Col. Keyes and Wade[13]. Returned home by sunset.

Monday 6th
Sent after Provisions and got None as we were like to march
that way today. However Sgt Tiffany and I walked out of
Camp and bought a Breakfast and a cheese. Returned and
packed up. Marched to Greenwich[14] and put up for the night
with eating a good supper so we lodged in the Courthouse[15].

---

the front rank". Thus formed, the company would then "perform the manual
exercise, and the wheeling's, marches, maneuvers, and firings...or as such
of them as shall be ordered". (de Steuben, Baron, *Regulations for the
Order and Discipline of the Troops of the United States,* J.Thomas and
E.T. Andrews, 1794)

[13] Col. Nathaniel Wade was captain of a local Ipswich, Massachusetts
militia at the start of the conflict with Great Britain and led his unit in pursuit
of British soldiers fleeing the battles at Lexington and Concord. Two
months later, the company served at Bunker Hill. Col. Wade would
ultimately command troops throughout the Rhode Island campaign, as well
as at Long Island, Harlem, and White Plains, New York. On September 25,
1780, Wade was appointed the Command of West Point. (MSSRW, Vol.
16, pp. 373-374)

[14] Refers to what is presently called East Greenwich, the town originally
named for the English counterpart when founded in 1677. In 1741 it was
divided between East and West, though many Rhode Islanders continued
to record the original 'Greenwich' in letters and diaries.

[15] The Courthouse on Main Street in East Greenwich was erected
sometime after 1752 when the committee who oversaw the construction
requested, and received permission to hold a lottery and raise funds to
finish the project. The courthouse, constructed three stories high on the
hillside, with its grand façade with twin peak gables and impressive colonial
cupola, would have provided ample room for the fifty-six men in the
company.

Tuesday 7th
Awoke and found a pleasant morning so we walked the Street to find where to Breakfast findly eat where we did last night then marched to Warwick Neck[16] where the Company crossed over the River[17]. However I stayed with the baggage as the wind would not permit to cross to Warren[18] the latter part of the Knight.

---

[16] In early January 1776, the Rhode Island General Assembly ordered that "a number of men, not exceeding fifty" be stationed at Warwick Neck. These men were to be comprised of both the Artillery Company of the town, as well as minutemen. Colonel John Waterman was given command, establishing his headquarters at the Thomas Wickes house, located at the entrance to the Neck, and a substantial fort was constructed at the Point, with a battery of three guns facing Narragansett Bay. (Edward Field, *Revolutionary Defenses in Rhode Island: An Historical Account of the Fortifications and Beacons Erected uring the American Revolution* Providence, Preston and Rounds 1896) pp. 84-85

[17] Robinson refers to the Providence River, whose ending point into the Bay is actually a bit north at Conimicut.

[18] The town of Warren, lying south of Barrington, and north of Bristol was among the first communities affected by the war. The residents suffered the most serious attack on the day of May 25, 1778 when a force of some 500 men, made up of the British 22nd light regiment, additional companies, and Hessian chasseurs landed before daybreak on Rumstick Point, roughly halfway between Bristol and Warren, and finding no resistance, marched into town. The soldiers harranged and roughed-up the villagers, disabled the town cannon, and marched to their main purpose, the large cache of boats that local militia had gathered near the stone bridge on the Kickemuit River for the imminent American attack to reclaim Acquidneck Island. Once there, the British troops burned 50-60 boats on the bank of the river, and captured twenty carpenters. They burned stores of pitch and tar, and the Baptist Church with several other buildings, before moving on to present-day Bristol.(see Desmarias, Norman *The Guide to the American Revolutionary War in Canada and New England,* Ithica, Busca Inc. 2009) p. 150

Wednesday 8th

Last night bunked aside the hay stacks. Tary'd by the stacks today. At night crossed with our baggage over to Warren Town. Found Capt. Richardson's company and bunked in for the knight[19].

Thursday 9th

This morning unloaded our baggage out of the Boat then paraided and Marched to Swansey[20] and took barrak in Capt Shearborne's house[21].

[19] The crossing was likely about halfway along the eastern side of Warwick Neck, where Rocky Point is located today. It lay across the "Providence Bay" from a small battery erected on Fort Hill in present day Warren about two miles south of the entrance to the Warren River, along the road to Bristol and Poppasquash Point.

[20] Located at the mouth of the Taunton River, the town of Swansea was named by settlers for the Welsh town of their origins. Original settlers included William Brenton, who had purchased much of the land, which would include parts of Barrington and Rehobeth from the indigenous peoples. It was incorporated in 1667 shortly after the First Baptist church of Massachusetts established itself in the settlement.

[21] Colonel Henry Sherburne began his service in the war as a Major in Church's Rhode Island Regiment, consisting of seven companies from Bristol and Newport counties. These were adapted into the Continental Line on 14 June 1775, reorganized, and then assigned to Greene's Brigade for the campaign in Roxbury. Many of the officers and soldiers of this brigade became members of the 1st and 2nd Rhode Island Continental line. Sherburne would be appointed Major of the 15th Continental line in January 1776, and in May be captured by Native Americans aligned with the British in the Battle of the Cedars, near Montreal, Canada. After release he would distinguish himself at the Battle of Trenton in December 1776. The following year he was given command of his own Regiment, consisting troops enlisted from Rhode Island, Massachusetts, and Connecticut. (*The Biographical Cyclopedia of Representative Men of Rhode Island* Providence, National Biographical Publishing Co. 1881 pp. 150-151, see also Heitman, p. 494)

Friday 10th
Pleasant weather so I got my clothes washed. I walked down
to Fall River and saw my friends in Capt. Richardson's
company. Returned before Sun Set.
Saturday 11th
Before noon had orders to March so we packed up and
Marched to Tiverton back of Watupper Ponds[22] about 3 miles
and took barraks in M. Burders[23] house.
Sunday 12th
Wet weather so we at the W.M. Burders at night we set off
after provisions however got none.
Monday 13th
Lousy morning however men went after provisions again.
Afternoon Capt. Stp Richardson[24] and Lt. Robin Bishop[25] came
to our barrak, so I saw my Uncle & heard from home and all
were well. So no more today....

---

[22] Located in present-day Fall River, Massachusetts, the two Watuupa
ponds are connected by "the Narrows", a thin strip of land that forms part
of the border between Fall River and Westport. At the time of Robinson's
service the whole of South Watuppa Pond lay within the borders of
Tiverton, as well as a third of the 4.2 mile long Watuppa Pond.

[23] Burder's house was likely one of the two homes along the road to Fall
River shown in an Army Corp of Engineer map from 1819 as belonging to
B. Burder and Abe Burder. They were located about a quarter of a mile
above the Quaker Meeting House, and perhaps a mile above the first of
two redoubts established above "the Gut", a narrow channel that separated
the mainland from Quacutt Neck.

[24] Captain Stephen Richardson was Captain of an Attleboro Militia
Company, which is said to have marched after the alarm of April 15, 1775,
took part in the Battle of Bunker Hill and the six-week campaign in Roxbury
from December into January 1776. He served again, according to records,
in October, November, and twelve days into December of 1776 as Captain
of the 4th Company in Colonel John Daggetts regiment. He was then
chosen to serve in the "the expedition to Rhode Island" in April 1777 until
May 15, 1777. He marched again from Attleboro on September 25th with
Robinson and the others of his company under command of Col. George
Williams. (MSSRW, Vol. 13, p. 265)

[25] Likely Nathaniel Bishop of Attleboro, who first served as Lieutenant in

Tuesday 14th

Last Evening had a play on the grass with the officers. This morning paraded & exercised awhile then had orders to march the Regt. and we had a long exercise got home about two o'clock pm. Officers had orders to meet at headquarters. Dur. Afternoon some Attleboro men came to Capt. Richardson's quarters & brought news all the militia were coming to join the army.

Wednesday 15th

Pleasant weather I feel some(what) unwell with a cold however crept(?) about

Thursday 16th

We had marching orders so we marched to the Col and drawd cartridges then marched on our way to Foglons Ferry[26]. So we marched within about half a mile of four corners[27] where Guards were drafted in order to Attack the Island however orders come to the contrary se we lodged in the wood.

Friday 17th

Capt. Moses Willmarth's company on the alarm of 9 April 1775. He would later serve with Col. John Daggets 4th Bristol Company, of which Capt. Alexander Foster's company marched at the alarm on Rhode Island, and was stationed there for twenty-five days from December 8, 1777. (MSSRW, Vol. 2, p. 22)

[26] Fogland Ferry lay at the southernmost tip of Tiverton, directly across from the British redoubt and barracks at Sandy Point on the shore of Aquidneck Island (Newport), which the British had occupied since December 8, 1776.

[27] A committee made up of residents of Puncatest and Seconnet, drew up thirty building lots, and a mill lot along Borden Brook and laid out Tiverton's "Four Corners" in 1710. The village grew in importance as travel and commerce flowed to the Fogland Ferry and the southern end of Tiverton expanded in the mid 18th century. (*Historic and Architectural Resources of Tiverton, A Preliminary Report*, Rhode Island Historic Preservation Committee, 1983, pp. 8-10)

Awoke and marched to Ladds tavern[28] about half a mile then had orders to march back again as I suppose to Imbody(?) in order to go on the island, however had orders again to go to quarters for the night.

Saturday 18th

Last night barraked at Mr. Cainan Gifford's house[29] where we had good Rum. This morning awoke and went after provisions in the Rain. At night heard Genl. Washington had a general battle with and defeated em' greatly. Heard Genl. Sullivan was slain…[30]

Sunday 19th

Pleasant morning. Had orders to March by 9 o'clock. Likewise we did and got in order to attack the Island at Night marched down to the water in order to embark where I saw Capt. Richardson's company however by some misfortune we did not attack the island so we returned to barrak[31].

---

[28] This is likely the tavern that was established near Tiverton Four Corners in 1749. There was a tavern also established early on, around The Gut. (*Ibid*)

[29] Caanan Gifford was born June 15, 1731 in Little Compton, the town where he would spend his entire life. He married Abigail Sallsbury of the town in June 1751. They had four children before her death in 1765. By the time of Robinson's visit, Gifford was a middle-aged man with a second wife, Martha Wilbur, and a household of four children; ranging from Ruth, his twenty-one year old daughter, to his five year old son, Noah Gifford. It must have been a bustling household. Gifford died in Little Compton on June 25, 1786 (or 1789), depending upon the source. (Gifford, Harry Elsworth *Gifford Genealogy 1626-1896* Wollostan, Mass. Pinkham Press 1896 p.20, Steve Condacure's New England Genealogy Index, Family Pages, 137.

[30] Unfounded camp rumors were the constant annoyance of Washington and his Officers during the war. Washington had in fact, continued his retreat toward Valley Forge after losing the battle at Germantown on 4, October 1777. John Sullivan had led one of the flanking columns during the American attack, and despite having to retreat when his troops ran low on ammunition, he was not wounded and was very much alive. Sullivan would be placed as Commander of the forces in the campaign to retake Acquidneck Island the following year.

Monday 20th

Pleasant morning. I went and got my shoes mended. Nothing strange today.

Tuesday 21st

Last night lodged in a bed. Awoke and found a rainy morning-got breakfast & helped make a return of the company. Then went down to Captain Stephen Richardson's company and saw my friends. Returned and had a merry evening with singing Capt. Richardson's song (Burgoyne is ours, Burgoyne is ours, the Island we'll have…etc.[32]) and returned to bed.

Wednesday 22nd

Cool morning. Afternoon marched down to the Capt's and attended roll call[33].

---

[31] That evening, according to British Major Frederick Mackenzie's diary, some 200 militiamen had gathered at Howland's Neck and at about midnight, began firing at two Hessian guards and six sentries posted at the bridge. The British returned fire and then retreated when an 18 pounder on Windmill Hill began firing at them as well. The brief engagement lasted all of twelve minutes. The following morning, British Scouts found several hats and bayonets left behind by the militias. (*Diary of Frederick MacKenzie Giving a Daily Narrative of his Military service as an Officer of the Royal Welch Fusiliers During the Years 1775-1781 in Massachusetts, Rhode Island and New York* Cambridge, Mass.: Harvard University Press 1930)

[32] Invading the northern colonies via Canada, British General John Burgoyne had routed the American troops at Ticonderoga, and appeared to have an easy march ahead of him to Albany, and ultimately, to the Hudson River. Militiamen using geurilla tactics stalled his momentum and gave the Americans time to gather reinforcements. Burgoyne would lose a battle at Benson Heights on October 7th, and then surrounded, the General would surrender his entire army at Saratoga on October 17, 1777.

[33] "According to Von Steuben's manual regarding The Rolls, a roll call was to be called at the beating of the drum to call the entire regiment at reveille, and "at noon, the commanding officers of companies shall cause the roll of their respective companies to be called, the men parading for that purpose without arms, and to be detained no longer than is necessary to call the roll". (von Steuben, Baron Frederick William, *Regulations for the Order and Discipline of the Troops of the United States. To Which is Added, An Appendix, Containing, the United States Militia Act, Passed in Congress, May 1792* Boston, I.Thomas & E.T. Andrews 1794, Dover Fascimile 1985)

Thursday 23rd

In the morning marched down to the Capt.'s for roll
call…Nothing strange till just dark when we had orders to
march with three days provisions. Then we marched to
Tiverton near Maj. Gedd's in order to go onto island, however
Not so marched back for quarters.

Friday 24th

Cloudy morning; today nothing strange until dark when Maj.
Clays found some of the Taunton men playing cards & he
burndt them immediately.

Saturday 25th

Wet morning & looks likely for a rainey day. Nothing strange
today.

Sunday 26th

Lousy morning. Nothing strange till Night when we had
orders to parade by 8 o'clock… We did in the dark and rain
and marched three or four miles then had orders to the right
about face so we returned home…

Monday 27th

Wet morning so we kept our barrak and made apple pie. At
night made a return of the company.

Tuesday 28th

Very rainy day so we kept our barrak and eat apple
pie…however a sick man went home in the rain.

Wednesday 29th

Lousy cold morning & I feel some(what) unwell with a flux.
However for the disease had boiled milk for breakfast.

Thursday 30th

A long storm seems to be somewhat over-and I seem to be
some what attended with a Flux. Towards night we packed up
& marched to Tiverton near Col. Gray[34]and took barrak in a
school house[35].

Friday 30th
cool morning. Nothing strange.

November 1st 1777
Saturday
Behold this is a day & very pleasant morning but as cold as pleasant. I first carried in a provision return for Capt. Richardson's company, took orders, etc. At night a small schooner come up the river against our barrak & dropt anchor[36].

Sunday 2nd.
Pleasant morning. our men are very hungry this morning having no bread however drawd one days allowance of flour before night... A man died with the ...distemper today at Mr. Philip Gray's[37] near our schoolhouse.

---

[34] Likely the large and elegant house of Col. Pardon Gray, which sat back from the main road from Fall River and Dartmouth. The house still stands today beside the Pardon Gray Preserve off Rt. 177.

[35] No early schoolhouse is mentioned in the historical survey of the town. It was likely a structure of little significance as Henry Barnard (1811-1900) would write in his pioneering treatise on the early "little red schoolhouse" he found in every village: "... standing in disgraceful contrast with every other structure designed for public or domestic use". It was likely accommodations little better than a barn.

[36] The encampment was along the Pocasset River (now Sakonnet) above the crossing where the stone bridge, first built in 1795, has now long been located.

[37] Philip Gray was born 22 June 1750 in Tiverton. He would marry Deborah Bailey of Little Compton in April 1768. They would raise eight children at their home, four of whom would have been living under the same roof as the soldiers, including the youngest at that time, Philip Junior; who in November 1777 was exactly one year old. Gray is listed on the 1777 Military Census as a private in Col. Isaac Cook's regiment and was the brother of Pardon Gray who served as a Lt. Colonel for the Tiverton Company. (Arnold, James N *Vital Records of Rhode Island 1636-1850* Providence, Narragansett Historical Publishing Co. 1901) Vol. 4 p. 84, Raymond, Marcius Dennison *Gray Genealogy, Being a Genealogical*

Monday 3rd.
Fine weather this morning. Drawd meat and bread. Hear good news from Genl. Washington[38]. Nothing happened strange today.

Tuesday 4th
Pleasant morning. I first made a weekly return and took details…Afternoon went to Mr. T.G.…to flasking[39] and eat supper there.

Wednesday 5th.
A warm morning, however we soon had orders to March so we packed up and marched from our school house about 10 o'clock to the boats and embarked on board and put off for Warren town-and arrived there about 9 o'clock pm and took barrak at Mr. Edward Eddy's house[40] and tarried the night.

Thursday 6th
Rainy morning. bought a breakfast at Mr. Eddy's however it cost me but three shillings & two (pence) for supper .

Record and History of the Descendants of John Gray, of Beverly, Massachusetts Tarrytown, New York 1897) p. 263, *!777 Military Census of Rhode Island*

[38] This is likely the news that troops under Col. Christopher Greene of Rhode Island had successfully fended off a Hessian attack on Fort Mercer at the battle of Red Bank, 22 October 1777.

[39] Flasking refers to the term for the process of making a wax mold for dentures.

[40] Edward Eddy had been drafted and served in Captain Ezra Ormsbee's Militia for the town in 1776. At the time of the troops barracking in his house, he seems to be running an ordinary or rooming house, but he later appears on the List of Captain Curtis Cole's Company of Colonel Nathan Millers Regiment in 1781.(Baker, Virginia *The History of Warren, Rhode Island in the War of the Revolution 1776-1783* Warren, privately published, 1901) pp. 38, 41, 46

Friday 7th

Awoke and found a fair morning. I had leave to go home so I packed up and crossed Thillings[41] Ferry from Warren and marched to Hunts[42] in Rehobeth and got breakfast then marched on homeward and got home about 5 o'clock am and found the folks well. Heard Mr. J. Perry was dead[43]-So I got dinner and shifted my clothes. Towards night Dr. Stanley came to our house so I saw him: in the evening I walked over to Mr. Pullens[44], then home and got supper, then walked down to Uncle J. Stanley's who was sick abed but getting better. From thence to Mr. Wm Stanley[45]'s where I met a number of younger gentlemen and ladies so we spent the evening in frivolity (?) then I returned home and went to sleep.

---

[41] This was likely Kelley's Ferry, which at the time of the Revolution lay on the northern end of Warren, while Carr's Ferry lay to the south. The location is at the end of Kelley Street today, just before the bridge to Barrington.

[42] The Proprietor was Daniel Hunt Jr. (1712-1781) whose father had established the tavern in 1724. He was married to Patience Wheaton Hunt (1714-1782).

[43] Jasiel Perry (1682-1777), the son of Samuel Perry of Rehobeth. Jasiel had married into the Willmarth family with his wedding to Rebecca Peck Willmarth in January 1706 and with her had four children. He was ninety-six at the time of his passing. (Burleigh, Clarence Herbert *Family File series, Percy and allied families,* Queen's University Archives, Queens University, Toronto, p. 5

[44] James Pullen (1749-1829) married Elona Capron at an unknown date, and with her had two children. He later married Phebe Stanley (1752-1821), who bore him nine children between 1776 and 1797. (ancestry.com)

[45] William Stanley (1720-1806) of Attleboro married Zilpha Daggett, widow of Comfort Smith in 1752 and was the father of Phebe Stanley. He was a founder of, and began keeping extensive notes on the Falls Burial Ground on Towne Street in the 1750's and would have been at Noah's funeral in 1788. He too would be buried there on his death in 1806.(Records of the Town of North Attleboro, Robinson Cemetery Records, Find A Grave Memorial # 74884377)

Saturday 8th

Awoke and got breakfast then went round the neighborhood and saw my kindred and friends. Returned home at night.

Sunday 9th

A rainy morning. However I went to Meeting and heard Mr. Welds preach[46]. Come home at night and eat supper, then walked over to Mr. Fuller's and read the news print.

Monday 10th

I awoke and found a rainy morning so I went to Mr. Drappers for leather, to Mr. Carpenters & back to Uncle B. Stanley[47] and got his mare and rode to Mr. J. Freeman[48]'s where I had the promise of having some shoes made. I also heard Genl. Howe and his army had surrendered themselves into the hands of Gen. Washington.

Tuesday 11th

---

[46] Rev. Habijah Weld was the third minister of Attleboro, ordained as pastor of the First Church on October 1, 1727, and served in that position for over fifty years. A description from the New England Genealogical Register fits the period when Robinson would have seen Weld preach: "Mr. Weld was of lower middle stature, and in the latter part of his life, corpulent. His constitution was vigorous, and his mind almost singularly energetic". (Daggett, John *A Sketch of the History of Attleborough* Dedham, H. Mann, Printer 1834 p. 56)

[47] Benjamin Stanley (1729-) was the older brother of Robinson's mother Deborah.

[48] James Freeman served in Captain Stephen Richardson's Company of Daggett's regiment. He would serve from 1775-1777 in Capt. Butler's Company, Lieut. Col. Thomas Nixon's 4th regiment, and Capt. Samuel Cowell's company of Col. Benjamin Hawes regiment. He would end his service and return to Attleboro on October 30, 1777. (MSSRW, Vol. 6, p. 41)

Fair cold weather…In the afternoon was at Deacon Stanley's and saw him who was getting better. Returned home for dinner-in afternoon was at Mr. Fuller's an hour or two. Toward night made a fire in the schoolhouse in order for singing school In the evening had a school and song then stayed & concluded the evening in playing cards.
Wednesday 12th
Cold morning so I walked round the neighborhood and saw my friends. Returned home at night.
Thursday 13th
Today I was getting ready to march in the evening. Went and saw E. Bacon and played cards. Returned home again late.
Friday 14th
Awoke early and packed and eat breakfast and marched on for Warren and overtook R. Stanley[49] agoing to Providence. So I walked with him four or five miles and parted about noon. I sat down by the way side and eat upon a chicken, which I had in my pack then marched and arrived at Warren about 3 o'clock pm found the company well barraked.
Saturday 15th
I awoke and crossed Thilley's Ferry and Brought some Milk and Cyder and Returned and got Breakfast,
-Drawd Lowance (?) Afternoon(,) crossed the Ferry and bought some Cyder and returned and eat supper- and Maj. Munro was at our Quarters.
At night our Mess was threatened…(?)
Sunday 16th

---

[49] Rial (or Royal) Stanley (1759-1817) of Attleboro was Robinson's cousin and served as a fifer in Capt. Jacob Ide's company of Daggett's regiment, and later as a drummer in Capt. Enoch Robinson's company. He was encamped in Rhode Island several times during his years of service including four months detached from his militia and encamped under Capt. Samuel Fisher. (MSSRW Vol. 14, p. 829)

Awoke and got Breakfast then went down to the Mills to push off boats- Returned and crossed Thilley's Ferry and Bought some Cyder and home again and had Roast Beef for diner. A comfortable Day is past.

Monday 17th

Awoke and went down to the water and helpt (bring?) down a bridge and got a Dram and returned and got breakfast And three of my 4 mess mates sett off home. However it snowed and Israel Hatch[50] was at our quarters. Towards night went over the Ferry with Sgt. Munro[51] and I. Turner[52] and Bought some Cyder & Milk. returned and had Rice and Milk for Supper and soon Bundled in...

Tuesday 18th

---

[50] Israel Hatch owned several drinking and lodging establishments along the stagecoach line that linked Providence to Boston, including the famous White Horse Tavern where noted colonial dissidents met. At the time of the American Revolution, he had built the stately and elegant Hatch Tavern in Attleboro, and gained legendary status when Washington stayed and exchanged a broken shoe buckle with the owner. Hatch served briefly in the militia, but acquired the title of Colonel by the close of the war. He was appointed the first post-master of Attleboro in 1789.(Moxham, *Garrison House has Long, Colorful History* The Sun Chronicle, Attleboro, March 28, 2001, *New England Magazine,* NS Vol. 11, OS Vol. 17 Sept 1894-February 1895 p. 232)

[51] Sergeant Samuel Munro served in Capt. Caleb Richardson's company after his enlistment in 1777. He would be promoted to Captain later that year. (MSSRW, Vol. 11, P. 212)

[52] Isaiah Turner of Wrentham initially served in a regiment raised in Suffolk and York counties. He was among the troops who marched to Warwick in the spring of 1776, and later served in the state with Capt. Samuel Fisher's Company, and in Capt. Ezekial Plimpton's company during September and October 1777. He is listed as discharged 28, October from service in Rhode Island, so his role at the time of meeting Robinson remains unclear. He would later serve as Corporal in a detachment under Lt. Jonas Temple, and again with Capt. Samuel Fisher's 4th Suffolk Co. before being discharged in 2 August 1780.(MSSRW, Vol. 16, p. 168)

Awoke and made cakes and tea for breakfast and Sgt. Munro and I. Turner went to breakfast with us, then went down to Bristol after provisions. Returned & dined with Sargeant Munro upon Pot (?) of fouls No more stranger…[53]

Wednesday 19th

This morning Sgt. Tiffany had a chat with a priest, M. Tomfor(?)

Our Company Beforenoon was sent Round Bristol[54] with boats however I stayd at home & spent the Day Chiefly in Writing. Toward night I cut up some wood and Sgt. Tiffany went over the ferry after Milk (& ccc).

When he returned we had milk for supper then sat and conversed about the present ladies, (etc.)

---

[53] This is likely Pot Eu Feu, a dish traditionally made with inexpensive cuts of beef, cooked for a lengthy time and then stewed with all manner of root vegetables.

[54] Dr Robert Honeyman wrote of the town in 1775, "Bristol is about half way between Providence and Newport, the whole distance being 30 miles. It is a small town lying on the East side of the river, & has some trade…" As with Warren, the town would be seriously affected by the conflict with Great Britain. A first attack came on October 7, 1775 when British Captain JamesJames Wallace bombarded the town when its residents refused to send a delegation to eet his demands for provisions. As the *Newport Mercury* in its October 9th edition: "Saturday afternoon the ships *Rose*, *Glascow*, and *Swan*". all armed vessels, "weighed anchor and went up the river, entered the harbour at Bristol, and demanded three hundred sheep, which not being complied with between 8 and 9 o'clock they began a heavy fire on said town and continued it upwards of an hour…" The town also suffered during the raid of May 25, 1778 when troops that had pillaged Warren continued on to Poppasquash, and then to Hope Street in the town and burned upwards of thirty houses and other buildings including the Episcopal Church, which the British mistakenly believed to be the location where the local militia stored their arms and gunpowder. In fact, a decree from the town council on 22 April 1775 that addressed the powder "lately had from Providence", and ordered that "Benjamin Bosworth take into custody the powder, balls, flints, etc., and deposit them in the court house in the closet under the stairs which had been fitted for that purpose". Other sources claim that St. Michael's church was also a repository for ammunition. (see Desmarias, *The Guide to The American Revolutionary War*…pp. 150-151.

Thursday 20th

Behold. This is a Day appointed as a Day of Thanksgiving to God throughout the State of Massachusetts Bay.
However, I being a soldier in the state of Rhode Island to keep in memory the memorable day, we arose and had tea for breakfast. I then went to Bristol after provisions and though some fatigue got it on board a boat and set off for Warren with Capt. Richardson and Mr. Goff and got in to Warren before night (,) and Sergt. Tiffany had a genteel supper cooked and Capt. Richardson and Lt. Jones went to supper with us, in the evening went down to Capt. Richardson's quarters, and though we had not Polley to kiss we had Black Bettey[55]& home to bed.

---

[55] While regiments of the Continental Line often had a number of women in camp to provide cleaning, laundering, cooking, and other services, militia units were largely on their own. Ladies visiting camps were always a welcome, if sometime unhealthy diversion from the monotony of camp life.

Friday 20th
Behold. This is the Day after Thanksgiving & I awoke of the flower[56] and got breakfast and the Major part of the Company went off with boats to Providence. However I stayd at home and before night Gen. Cornell[57] was in Warren and ordered that Guards were kept out properly…And to conclude I was for Guard tonight…

Saturday 22nd

---

[56] An expression used to describe drunkenness. Robinson describes himself several times in the journal as "on the flower", though in this case, he appears to have woken up still somewhat tipsy. When Benjamin Franklin collected terms for drunkenness for his Almanac, he discovered more than two hundred expressions for the common vice throughout the colonies.

[57] General Ezekiel Cornell was born 27 March 1732/33 and by the time of his service in the American Revolution, had acquired the nickname of "Old Snarl". He served as lieutenant colonel in Hitchcock's regiment, and took part with his company in the Siege of Boston, and the battle of Bunker Hill. He spent his early career rooting out royalists on Long Island, and was also part of the Continental Army contingent that arrested loyalist and New York mayor David Matthews on 22 June 1776, on suspicion of being involved with a plot to kill Washington. By the time of the review of Robinson's company, Cornell had been appointed Brigadier General of the Rhode Island troops, and would have an active role in the Battle of Rhode Island, 29 August 1778. (Rev. John Cornell, *Geneology of the Cornell Family: Being an Account of the Descendants of Thomas Cornell*, New York, T.A. Wright Publishers, 1902)

Very warm and pleasant. At 9 o'clock was relieved from guard. Afternoon set off for Bristol for provisions…coming back shot some fowl and landed with our bread before night. Capt. Richardson was absent. Lt. Fuller brought some ointment (etc.)

A number of Taunton men came in at Night…

Sunday 23rd

Pleasant morning & the troops best guard were paraded---in the forenoon heard Mr. Tompson preach – Afternoon crossed the Ferry after cyder and something of a carnal disease passed on…Returned back and in the evening Sergt. Tiffany and I anointed with Lt. Fuller's ointment[58].

Monday 24th

I awoke and took the care of Kickimuit Guard. Drawd Lowance to Day. However at Night I went to Coll. Chiles' borrowed some bread (hard biscuts) and Drank some Grogg. Returned and eat supper and Sergt. Tiffany and I did as last night(viz anointed) and went to bed on the flower…

Tuesday 25th

This morning was relieved from Guard, in the forenoon I went over the Ferry and got some milk & cyder. Afternoon was at Bristol after provisions. returned to eat supper then went to Squire Coles[59] and bought some Grogg and in the evening Sergt. Tiffany & I took the third watch by the fire and drank Rum & Brimstora in a great plenty and concluded in jollity& then to bed.

Wednesday 26th

---

[58] Venereal Disease was among the most common diseases to afflict the troops during the war. Lt. Fuller's ointment likely held ingredients that included arsenic, mercury, and sulphur, all commonly known cures during the eighteenth century.

[59] Coles ran a hotel on the corner of Main and Joyce Streets in Warren from 1762. The hotel burned in 1893.

Awoke and drank a morning toast of Grogg & (saffron?) and got breakfast. Capt. Richardson came in to camp & in the evening the Capt. and Lt. Fuller was at our quarters and a jolly discourse past on…After that I spent some time in writing.

Nothing more memorable happened today so Good Night…

Thursday 27th

Awoke and took Kickemuit Guard[60], nothing happened singular until Dark when Capt. Richardson asked Sergt. Tiffany and I to supper with him. We attended at his quarters where we found a Roast Turkey and a supper cooked with the most splendor circumstances would (permit). Wine & Cyder was very plenty. So we sat down and eat with the Commanding officers then returned home and being on guard spent part of the night reading.

Friday 28th

I awoke and was released from Guard so I spent the day part writing, part in reading eating & drinking cyder etc.

Capt. Richardson crossed in a boat to North Kingstown[61]. Sergt. Tiffany set out (for) home. Want bread very much(,) however drawd five loaves for our Company.

The day is past and I am the same wretch…

Saturday 29th

Awoke and had supper for breakfast- Stews Crowd's for Dinner without bread. Crowd's for supper again with an Indian cake baked in the apples[62].

---

[60] Guards were placed along the banks of the Kickemuit River, most prominently at both banks at Bristol Narrows, the entry to the river from Mount Hope Bay. The river was a key supply artery throughout the war.

[61] Richardson likely sailed down the Warren River past Poppasquash Point, and then tacked West-South-west to reach North Kingstown, or Updike's harbor, at present day Mill Cove, just offshore of the Plantation house, and northeast of present day Wickford harbor.

[62] As indelicate as twenty-first century readers may find it, dishes made

I spent much of the day reading the Arabian Nights entertainment. At night Lt. Fuller was at our quarters and I was- for Guard tomorrow.

Nothing more strange however a very rainy day is past and I'm the same wretch...

Sunday 30th

Lousy morning. However we had Supper for breakfast and then took the care of the guard, etc...

This day I spent some in reading & writing but more in eating & drinking & in the evening I was at Lt. Fuller's quarters and suppd with him and read some of Mr. Harry's works.

Monday December 1st 1777

Behold this is the first day of December and Capt. Richardson returned from O.P. Newtown[63] in the sailboat. About six of us immediately then embarked for Bristol and drawed allowance and put back for Warren and arrived at the wharf about dark and unloaded our provisions and got supper & Sergt. Tiffany had returned.

Dec. 2nd 1777 Tuesday

---

with crow were a common cuisine of poor Europeans, and survived the journey to America. One of the more popular recipes was a "crow casserole," a dish made with crow breasts, bacon, onion, and topped by sauerkraut. Curiously, Robinson mentions apple cake for desert, as one dish made with the birds eveolved into an open-faced pie made with apples and called a "crows nest" .

[63] Reference to Updike's or Opdykes Newtown, land owned by the Updike family and which town was laid out by Captain Lodowick Updike between 1709-1715. By the time of the American Revolution, the town was still referred to by this name, although Updike's choice of Wickford had also taken hold. The town maintained an active port during the Revolution, and when the British attempted to raid the town in 1776, the single cannon commissioned by the General Assembly for the town's defense, and the firing of guns by local militia managed to fend them off. (Updike, Wilkins *A History of the Episcopal Church in Narragansett, Rhode Island Including a History of other Episcopal Churches in the State* Boston, Merrymount Press 1907)

Awoke and went down to the Capts where I spent the day in helping make Abstracts[64] with the Capt. and Lt. Fuller-where we drank wine & cyder in great plenty.

Returned home at night to my lodging and got supper and turned for the night…

Nothing remarkable happened….

Wednesday 3rd.

Very cold etc. However I was on Guard and had cyder plenty as two barrels were brought into mess yesterday.

I spent the day mostly in reading & writing- heard ensign Sweetland[65] was very sick and was not like to return to camp very soon.

Nothing strange today…

Thursday 4th

Awoke and wrote a letter and sent home. Made a report of my Guard…Afternoon went with Sergt. Tiffany to the Quarter Guard and saw Charity Weave[66] & returned and eat supper and wrote awhile and turned in for the night.

---

[64] Making card abstracts was to organize the compilation of military service records, including muster rolls, pay rolls, and returns; and from these, meticulously copy each individual soldier's information onto a type of index card.

[65] Bowen Sweetland, served as a private with Capt. Jabez Ellis' company of Attleboro militia. He was among those called with the militia to Rhode Island, and served there until January 1, 1778. He would later serve in Capt. Samuel Robinson's company of Col. Wade's regiment, and in companies belonging to Colonels Thomas Carpenter and Isaac Dean's regiments. He was discharged August 8, 1780 and allowed two days travel to march from Tiverton to his home in Attleboro. (MSSRW, Vol. 15, pp. 298-299)

[66] Likely refers to a community weaving organized by local women to help clothe the troops. After Congresses appointment of a Commissioner to supply the Army, the Rounding up worn clothing, they would patch breeches and darn stockings as well as weave new cloth for both shirts and blankets.

Friday 5th
Nothing strange happened to Day only we had orders to
move from Mr. Tompson to where the Captain quarters
tomorrow.
So I spent the day in reading & writing, eating and drinking
cyder...and the day ends.

Saturday 6th
Cold morning, however I was on the K guard so we got
breakfast and moved down from Mr. Tompsons to the Chiles,
and took barrak and erected our bunks and drank cyder and
turned in for the night.
Sunday 7th
Very warm and pleasant morning, so I kept my barrak in the
forenoon. Afternoon I was to see Lt. Fuller and a very sedate
discourse passed while there.
Returned home and in the evening some reading, some
writing, some eating and drinking cyder passed on...and then
bed.
Monday 8th
Warm morning. Got breakfast and sergt. M. Louth being
absent, went on Kic...guard.
Before night Ensign Sweetland returned into camp who had
been sick at home...
Nothing remarkable happened today...
Tuesday 9th
Awoke and got breakfast and took the care of the Guard.
Before night Lt. Jones returned from home into camp & at
night I crossed over the Ferry after some milk however we got
none so we returned.
Nothing remarkable today happened...
Wednesday 10th
Awoke and returned the Capt's watch. Afterward saw C.
Richardson Jr[67]. who was sick with the measles.

Afterward went down to Kickemuit and helped draw boats, etc.

Returned home and very hungry and dined upon some peas and meat and turned in for the night.

Thursday 11th
Awoke and eat suppawn[68] for breakfast and three of my mess went home however Sergt. Tiffany cooked in I. Jackson's room[69].

Before noon set off to Bristol after provisions returning home bought ne a wig. Got home and on with my wig and drank cyder & got some (?) then divided the allowance and waked up and got ready for supper...

Friday 12th

---

[67] Caleb Richardson Jr. (1762-1838) enlisted as a fifier in Capt. Richardson's company of Walker's regiment in August 1775 serving 3 months and eight days at Roxbury until Oct 6th of that year. He later served as private in Captain Willmarth's company of Dean's regiment, marching to Rhode Island on July 31, 1780, and serving ten days there on alarm. Caleb married Huldah Hatch in June 1787, and would apply for a pension in September 1832 while living in Susquehannah County, Pa. He died there on June 30, 1838. (MSSRW Vol. 13, p. 230, U.S. Revolutionary War Pensions W8553),

[68] A thick porridge consisting of cornmeal and milk cooked on the stove until thickened.

[69] Isaac Jackson enlisted as a private in Captain Stephen Richardson's company of Attleboro militia April 21, 1777 and served in Rhode Island for nearly the whole of his military career, under Capt's Israel Trow of Col. Josiah Whitney's regiment, then Abiel Clap of the Bristol Company that year, and on September 12th 1777, was mustered into Col. Danforth Keye's regiment, for which he served three more months and twenty-one days in Rhode Island. He would later sign on for 21 days service with Capt. Caleb Richardson in the spring of 1779. (MSSRW, Vol. 8, p. 669)

Awoke and got breakfast and then I went on Kickemuit guard and Capt. Richardson went home and gave leave I might do likewise however I tarried with the guard today snd the time passed in jollility as we had wine and cyder to drink and (cole)slaw for supper and (?) then to bed.

Saturday 13th
This morning at six o'clock Capt. Fuller came and awakened me and Tripp turned out and (?) sentinels. After this, I soon awoke and eat breakfast of suppawn and gave the rear of the guard to Sergt. Tiffany & Hez. Then I packed up and marched for home. Got as far as Mr. Morter and drank some cyder then to Mr. Daggetts where I found a letter from E. Bacon[70]. Then home and found all well.

Sunday 14th
Awoke and got breakfast and set off to meeting and heard Mr. Welds preach and saw many of my old acquaintances and the fair sex....Returned home and got supper and walked to Mr. Pullen and saw I. Pullen who was very sick, then returned home with J. Stanley[71] and sang a few tunes and ended the day.

Monday 15th

---

[70] Edward Bacon (1715-1789) of Attleboro married Elizabeth Stanley of Rehobeth, 17 February 1742. They had three children, Joseph (1746-1777), Mary (1751-1771) and Ebenezer (1755-1816). (Arnold, James N. *Vital Record of Rehobeth 1642-1896 Vol. 3-4* Providence, Narragansett Historical Publishing Co. 1897) p. 352, Find A Grave Memorial # 57484895

[71] Likely his Uncle Jacob Stanley. Robinson also had an Uncle Jonathan, but he was more active in the war and seems to have been in New York at the time of Noah's visit.

Pleasant morning so I went up to Un. Mt. and got some leather for breeches

Then went to Mr. Drapers and saw the folks and had an invitation to keep school at Dedham[72].

Returned home and D.N.B. and E.Bn. come to our house then we went to schoolhouse to sing then to Mr. Wm Star where the girls was…

Tuesday 16th

In the forenoon E. Bacon went with me to Mrs. Barrows, I then went with him to Mr. Drowns. Came back to D. Stands and dined there, it then began to snow so I returned home at night. I went up to Mr. Daggetts and drank some cyder and eat apples and sang some tunes and returned home and turned in for the night.

NB saw some girls…

Wednesday 17th

I Breakfast and went to Deacon Stanleys and saw C.S. Lee. Returned home and Un. E Mtl (?) was at our house. Afternoon I was at Mr. Pullen(')s and saw_____. Returned home and stayd till night then went to Mr. Pullens[73] again and tarried awhile and returned home and got supper and turned in….

Thursday 18th

---

[72] Dedham's schoolhouse during these years would have been the structure built at the turn of the century, a twenty-foot by nineteen-foot clapboarded building with a stairway leading to a chamber above, and provided with a chimney. It was reportedly located on the hill near the Meting house, on what is now Winter Street. (*Dedham Historical Register* Vol. 6, p. 6)

[73] James Pullen Sr. (1720-1785) was born in Rehobeth and married Lydia Woodcock of Attleboro. Their sons James Jr.,(1749-1829) William, (1753-1821) Oliver, (1759-1840) and the youngest John, (1763-1810) who enlisted at seventeen, would all serve in the Revolutionary War. (Lythgoe, Darrin *Early Waterville, Me. Families, James Pullen (1720-1785)* http://watervillegenaology.com) see also MSSRW Vol. pp. 69, 70)

Behold this is a day set apart as a publick and continual Thanksgiving to God. So I awoke and C. Richardson came to my father's and brought orders for me to be in camp by ten o'clock tomorrow. So I got breakfast and rode in the rain to Ensign Sweetlands and gave him that same order then went to meeting and heard Mr. Welds preach then returned home and eat.

Eat the fat and Drank the sweet then repaired to the schoolhouse for a sing.

So we sang a few tunes and I had an invitation to keep….the school and provided house…..Jos. Draper Jr[74]. and Mrs Bn was my company so we spent the evening in jollity and I saw a large number of the (?) sex….

Returned to Mr. D's and put up Major Gort of Heights Hill, my Company…

Friday 19th

Returned home two or three hours before day and packed up and set off (for) Warren. Got as far as Mr. Barons and went to Ensign S window and awoke him and went in the house with him and drank egg cyder and parted. So I got into Warren about eleven o'clock and passed muster….

At night am very weary.

Saturday 20th

Very cold morning. awoke before sunrise and bailed out the scow then went on board her and put out for Providence however as the wind nor tide did not favor us we could not get up so we left her in a creek and returned home weary. However got supper and wrote awhile and bundled in for the night.[75]

---

[74] Josiah Draper Jr. (1753-1819) was born in Attleboro and was twenty-four at the time of this outing with his friend. He was the brother of Abigail Draper who would later marry Noah Robinson. Josiah would enlist as a drummer in Capt. Ezekial Plymton's company of Medfield, Massachusetts in September 1778. (Thomas Waln-Morgan Draper, *The Drapers in America: Being a History and Geneology of Those of That Name and Connection* (New York, Palmenus Printing Co. 1892 p. 78)

Sunday 21st

Awoke and got breakfast and put out for the scow but the wind and tide and sea running high we could not get up to Providence so we returned home again and spent the day in other recreation and employment.

Heard nor saw nothing remarkable....

Monday 22nd

Got breakfast and went onboard the scow again the third time and put off (for) Providence and through very hard fatigue and getting very wet we arrived at Providence about sunset and bought some bread and cheese and drawd some (portagee) Rum and drank very hearty and set off home to Warren and the musick went well as we were all part groggy...[76]

Tuesday 23rd

This morning awoke and remember yesterdays fatigue so we got breakfast and went up to the Captain's quarters and got some paper. Returned home again.

Spent some time in writing, etc. See none of my messmates. Some unwell, perhaps with the measles...at night kild crabs...

Wednesday 24th

Went on guard, however nothing remarkable happened. At night did as last night and turned in for (?) pm

Thursday 25th

---

[75] Flat-bottomed sailing scows were a popular boat for the region, having the distinct advantage of being able to navigate the shallow coves and rivers that extended from the coastline. Robinson and his co-horts efforts to cut through the current at the mouth of the Warren River and then position themselves to enter the narrow mouth of the Providence River just a few nautical miles north, and then past the known shoals and natural obstacles made the passage a challenge even with the tide and "favorable weather".

[76] One may note, that it took the crew an entire day to sail the roughly eleven nautical miles upriver.

Awoke and got breakfast. I concluded to have a bang[77] this evening and resolved to have the commodities which are needed in the page following:
The following articles were provided for at the bang:
Rum, Wine, Sugar, Eggs, Cyder.
So I went and wrote for the Capt. The major part of the day. Towards night returned home and eat super and about six o'clock drank one mug of Samfron then a mug of egg pop and walked up to the Capt's where we drank wine a great plenty…At eight o'clock returned home and the Capt & Lt. Jones with us, so we drank up what liquor we had. However Lt. Jones drawd another quart of wine and brought (it) in as a gift. So we drank liquor and…danced and evening passed in jollity…
Friday 26th
This morning awoke and found the fields covered with snow. However we did not rise very early this morning as last night's bang had not quite left us. However Capt. Richardson set off for Providence.
Nothing remarkable today.

Saturday 27th
Awoke and took the care of K…guard however I spent the major part of the day in writing
I might remember the topical tone of my messmates viz our times are out three days from tomorrow…thus the day ends.
Sunday 28th
Awoke and found a snowy morning, however was released from Guard.
It being very cold I did not go far from my barrak and the discourse was three days more…
Nothing remarkable happened.

---

[77] A general British slang term for "finding a thrill", Robinson's version seems to be a holiday party comprised of drinking concoctions made from what liquor he may acquire.

Monday 29th
Cold morning, so I walked round the town to find a horse to go to Bristol after provisions however I got none so they set off with a hand-sled.

Early hand-sleigh, dated 1788. Robinson would have used something similar to haul provisions.

I might remind that Lt. Fuller and Ensign Sweetland has been absent from camp these several days…
Tuesday 30th
Awoke and went up in the Capt's quarters where I spent the day in writing-however I have the care of the Guard.
At night Major Tiffany came in to camp with a sled. In the evening we received our warrant and drank grogg and returned home and turned in
Wednesday 31st
Awoke and returned in our pots and kitchen…Drawd some …money and eight dollars in wages.
Returned home what was borrowed and prepared for the ensuing day
I might remark the conduct of A. F. Lee how day after day they left their camp vy 7 o'clock at night…

Thursday 1st 1778

Behold the memorable year 1777 is now past and our service concluded for the present.

And thanks be to the Omnipotent Power who has preserved the poor object through the last year & campaign and may he look down & preserve the simple object the ensuing year 1778. May he learn thy will.

This morning I awoke and packed up and marched about (a) Day for home (fired a gun at the rising of the sun). Marched about five miles where we got breakfast at 4/0 per noon then marched on through Rehobeth where we got cyder &c the sun about two flowers high (near Capt. Willmarth). My messmates paraded and fired a volley & parted in peace.

I then marched on for G.S. where I got some victuals then to Uncle Capron[78] and stayed a while then for home again. Met J.D. & L.T. and gave them a gun then returned home and discharged my gun several times and found all well. Got supper and turned in for the night.

January 2, 1778 Friday

(I might first remark to the comment I heard last night returning home)

I got breakfast and went up to see Mr. Draper concerning keeping school and returned home(,) got dinner(,) and went to Dn Sr, where the Officers were, then Adj. Daggetts, then home.....

Saturday 3rd

---

[78] Elija Capron would marry Abigail Stanley. He served as Sergeant in Capt. Stephen Richardson's company of minutemen who answered the alarms at Lexington, and later Rhode Island. He also served as 2nd Lietenant in the 40th Bristol County regiment in 1779. He was born, lived, and died in Attleboro. (MSSRW Vol. 3, p. 84, Find A Grave Memorial # 31247382)

I got breakfast & went up (to) Adjt. Daggetts where I dined, then to Mr. N. Daggetts from thence to Mr. Barrows then to Uncle B. Stanley (,) from thence to the W. Bacons where I saw B.S. however I bought something for caper for my gown, then home of Mr. Pullen to read the print & home.

Sunday 4th

This day I went to meeting and heard Mr. Welds preach. Returned home and got supper...

I might remark the remainder of what happened but however I shall omit all onley DB

(page cut)

Monday 5th

I got breakfast and set off to Wrentham (in the snow) after some cloth, however I got none so I returned and A. R. came to our house and went with me to sing at No. Boston (?) (to Mr. Nancy's)

Tuesday 6th

Before noon Doc. Bliss[79] came to our house and dined. (T)hen I went home with him & tarried an hour or two then came back to Mr. Stanley's and saw B.S. (,) from thence to the schoolhouse then home and got supper & to the schoolhouse where we had a fine sing. (saw B.) (G)uile came home with me)

(page cut)

Wednesday 7th

---

[79] Dr. James Bliss (1757-1834) served as surgeon's mate with Col. Thomas Carpenter's regiment of militia, and also at the battle of While Plains Bliss began his own practice in Wrentham by 1789, and later moved to Rehobeth where he became a successful physician. He married Hannah Guild of Attleboro with whom he would have thirteen children, one dying in infancy, before her death in October 1816. He would later marry Sarah Deane of Dighton, Massachusetts. (Cutler, William Richard *New England Families, Genealogical and Memorial* Vol. 4 p. 1871, and Tilton, Rev. George H. *A History of Rehobeth, Massachusetts 1643-1918* Boston, Privately Printed, 1918 p. 323)

I went to Mr. Barrows & then to D. Stanley's.
In the evening was at D. Sand.
C.S. came home with me to brake some wool...
Nothing remarkable happened

Thursday 8th
This morning carried C.S. home and L.T. came to our house.
Towards night was at Mr. Pullens.
Returned home and Mr. J. Daman[80] came to our house and hired me to do his turn in the service-so he gave me forty-seven dollars and then to bed.

The End
Much more might have been recorded but it will be inserted in the next volume for the ensuing campaign
So no more....Finis

---

[80] John Daman of Attleboro was married to Annah Hunting sometime before 1758 when their first daughter Mary was born. The couple had five more children, two sons and three daughters to the clan, the youngest daughter Sarah being born August 24, 1776. Though he paid Robinson to serve in his place, he is listed as serving on the town's Committee of Safety in 1779. (*Vital Records of Attleboro,* Daggett, John *A Sketch of the History of Attleboro* p. 126)

Site of Kelley's Ferry, Warren, R.I. photo by the author

The Kickemuit River as it enters Mount Hope Bay.
photo by the author

Volume II: Noah Robinson's Book
Noah Robinson's Journal of his Intended Campaign by God's Permition: in Col. John Daggets Reg.
Raised by the State of Massachusetts in New England:
Col. Daggett's from Attleboro

January 8, 1778
Thursday
I arose and found some what wet so I got breakfast &
provided a horse and carried CS home and brought L… back
to my Father's…
(A town meeting today for Mr. Welds conferring his salary)
In the evening Mr. D was at our house and I engaged on
behalf of him in the three months service in Col. Dagget's
Regt.
Friday 9th
I arose very early and got breakfast and set off to Col.
Daggets. However I found him not at home so I came back to
Uncle E. Robinson[81]'s where Col. Dagget was and gave me the
promise of Doing his Writing and gave me leave to stay at
home until Tuesday and then march for the Regt.

---

[81] Enoch Robinson (1733-1798) was commissioned as 2nd Lieutenant with
Capt. Jabez Ellis' company of Attleboro militiamen on the march of 19 April

Nothing remarkable happened today however at Night I was up to Mr. P's for the sing & was at Mr. Maxays[82] where we drank flip…got home again about ten o'clock.

Saturday 10th

I arose and found a very pleasant morning so I sett off for Daggetts however I met him on horseback a Riding in to Camp…

Saw E. Daggett who informed me I was depended on to keep school in Dedham which had brought me into a primm(?) as I had engaged in the service. However went up to Mr. J.D. and cleared myself as well as I could-Saw Mrs A. & Molly Draper who were in good Plight..then home.

Sunday 11th

In the forenoon I was at Meeting and heard Mr. Thatcher preach. Afternoon, it being very snowy I tarried with Doc. Bliss until the folks came home from Meeting then I went home and got supper & walked as far as Uncle BS where I rode from to P. –

Where I spent the Night in Company with Mrs. (Beacon)…the Weather something stormy

Monday 12th

1775. He served as Lieutenant in Capt. Caleb Richardson's company of Walker's regiment later that year, also as 1st Lieutenant in Capt. Elisha May's 6th company and Capt. Abiel Clap's company of Daggetts regiment, whose company marched to Rhode Island 4 July 1777. He was unengaged at the time of his nephew's visit, but would return to the militia after being recommissioned on 29 July 1778 for six weeks of service with Capt. Samuel Robinson's company. He would serve again in Rhode Island, stationed for four weeks with Capt. Samuel Fisher's company, and a final time when he marched as Captain, with Col. Isaac Dean's company on 31 July 1780 to spend eight days in Tiverton. (MSSRW, Vol. 13, pp. 440-441)

[82] Maxcys tavern was originally the Woodcock Garrison House in present day Dighton, Massachusetts. The house was operated as a taven by its builder John Dagget, and then John Maxcy, and later, Israel Hatch, whose descendants would operate the tavern well into the 19th century. (MACRIS inventory for Woodcock-Daggett Garrison House, Commonwealth of Massachusetts, 2014)

I was at home about Sunrise (slept a nap) then went to Uncle E. Robinson's and borrowed his knapsack-then home & dined & went to Mr. DS. Saw BS-could not borrow a blanket So I went to Mr. Perry's whence I got a blanket-
Then went to E.D. and borrowed his gun & (?) Box… Went back to D.S. and Doc. Bliss went home with me
I was first at Mrs. Barrow's & was measured for clothes.

Tuesday 13th
This morning I arose Early and Packed up and got Breakfast and set off upon my Intended Campaigning by Gods permition-So I marched as far as Providence Where I found Capt. Willmarth's Company[83] and was informed that Col. Dagget had marched to Warwick. So I concluded to stay in Providence to Night and went and bought me some buttons at (?)
Saw Nothing remarkable However at Night I bunked in with my Brother[84] in ye work house….

Wednesday 14th
Pleasant morning so I got some victuals and marched off with Capt. W. for Warwick. Marched as far as Pawtuxet where we drank a mug of cyder & then marched on again about 4 miles to Warwick where I found Col. Daggett at Sgt. Warnes. I unflung my pack and Dined

[83] Moses Willmarth was Captain of the 9th Company of Col. Daggetts Regiment and served three months in Rhode Island from January 1, 1778. He would later serve in the state as Captain in Col. Thomas Carpenters regiment later that year, and with Col. Isaac Dean's regiment before his discharge on August 7, 1780. (MSSRW, Vol. 17, p. 526)

[84] Philip Robinson enlisted as private in Captain Moses Wilmarth's company of Daggetts Regiment, serving from January 1, 1778 through March, two months and twenty-five days in Rhode Island. He would later serve as Sergeant in Capt. Caleb Richardson's company of Hathaway's regiment, serving for twenty-one days from March 25, 1779. (MSSRW Vol. 13, p. 462)

Afternoon Capt. Willmarths Company came in to town o I went & saw 'em. Returned back to the Col. & in the evening I wrote of Genl orders…and song sometimes and turned in about 11 o'clock.

Thursday- January 15th

I arose and found a Cold morning. However I drank coffee for Breakfast and did some writing in the afternoon. (Wrote of some Regt. orders)

Afternoon three younger ladys come to Col. Daggetts Quar(ters) and two there was before which made up a pretty handsome sett. Towards Night I went to Capt. Willmarth's Company & drank cyder (Girls-2 more) Returned back and the Ladys drank coffee.

Friday 16th

A very cold morning However I drank coffee for Breakfast & etc. Then moved my pack to Capt Lippits[85] where the Cols are quartered and found not very good conveniences However I went to the store and Drawd some cooking utentils and Provisions and returned and dined upon a hunk of beef. Before Night Col. Daggett come to Warren and Brought word that the Adjt. child was sick so he went home…

Saturday- January 17th

Last night bundled on the flower with Col. Daggett Awoke and went with ED and paraded the Guards (Snow and Rain Wates upon the Day…)

---

[85] The Lippit Homestad (circa 1715) was one of the oldest houses in Warwick. For 33 years leading up to the Revolution it was inhabited by Jeremiah Lippit, the town clerk; and Warwick's records were kept on the premises. During this period, the four corners at the entrance to Warwick Neck were "The center of the community". The house at this time was commandeered for the use of the officers, along with the Wickes-Gardiner House, which sat directly opposite the entrance to the Neck, and where Col. Waterman and his officers were quartered. (Lane, Rev. William Hoyle, *An Interseting Chapter in the History of Rhode Island, An Old Story Retold* Shawomet, Privately Printed, 1926 courtesy of the Warwick Historical Society)

Afternoon I made out details and did some writing....At night it being very Rainey the Col. bundled on the flower.
Sunday 18th
This morning arose and did some writing & carried in a prisoners crime...
Had not much business in the forenoon- in the afternoon went to Capt. Will(marth's) & drank Cyder.
Returned home and eat Supper and Nothing Strange happened to Day.

Monday Jan. 19th
This morning arose and did some Writing. About Eleven o'clock had some rice for Breakfast.
Afternoon Col. Daggetts Regt. paraded for Exercise
Nothing Remarkable happened to Day.
Tuesday 20th
I had considerable writing to do. A Court Martial set at Capt. Willmarth's quarters.
At Night Adjt. Daggett came in to camp & brought comfortable News & two barrels of Cyder.
Wednesday 21st
In the fore part of the day I wrote considerable Afternoon several women came after papers to go on Board the Flagg & towards Night I rode down to the Point and carried some orders & Returned back[86].

---

[86] In January 1776 the General Assembly of Rhode Island had declared that "a number of men, not exceeding fifty, be stationed at Warwick Neck, including the Artillery Company in Warwick; the remainder to be minutemen". Col. John Waterman commanded the troops stationed there which over the course of the war would include the Kentish Guard, the Pawtuxet Rangers, the Scituate Rangers, and militia men from Massachusetts regiments. According to Edward Field, "a substantial work...was erected" and in addition to the fort, "a system of entrenchments ws laid out along the northerly side of the old road leading from Apponaug to Old Warwick". (Field, Edward *Revolutionary Defenses in Rhode Island* Providence, Preston & Rounds 1896) pp. 84-86

Eat a very good supper and felt very happy with my briefings and scrivening. The evening passed in jollity and so forth-
Thursday Jan 22nd
Arose and sealed up some letter and went up to the parade & was informed my brother was very much poisoned So I went and saw him then went to Col. Daggett & got a furlow for him and Mr. E. Daggett. Sett off (for) home together who carried a letter to Doctor B & one to Mrs. Bacon from their humble servant NR.
Afternoon had considerable writing to do, etc.
Col. Daggett went to Providence and back. Bought two barrels more of Cyder.
Friday 23rd
Pleasant Morning.
Today I wrote considerabley.
Adjt. & Q.M. moved their Quarters & c.
Nothing Remarkable happened.
Saturday 24th
Very Cold morning with some snow &c. Part of Capt. Willmarth's Company to Move to the Fulling Mills today &c[87]. One soldier discharged in Col. Daggetts regt. &c.
Nothing Remarkable happened in my Knowledge.
Sunday Jan. 25th 1778
Snowy this morning underfoot and overhead in the forenoon. Did not stur out much. after Noon went at Adjt. Daggets[88] Quart(ers). Towards night Capt. Randall[89] & Lt. Godfrey & Adjt. Daggett was at our quarters and we had a sing. In the evening the Field Officers went to the Gen(eral) and brought back some orders.

---

[87] Likely the fulling mills of Moses Lippit that were located at the opening of Buckeye brook to Narragansett Bay, located at the end of Economy Ave. where Lippit's house still stands today.

[88] Elihu Daggett was Adjutant in Col Daggetts regiment from 2 January 1778, until April of that year. He would also serve in Rhode Island with Brig. Gen, Ezek Cornell brigade and be Adjutant for Col. Isaac Dean's regiment, which included service in Tiverton. (MSSRW, Vol. 4, p. 355)

Lt. Col. Hathaway is Appointed Officer of Day tomorrow.
Monday 26th
Very cold morning. However I agreed to go the Rounds to
Night with Lt. Col. Hathaway & Adjt. Daggett.
This afternoon was confined three Chases &c. A Carpenter
came and built us Slaw bunks. At Night bunked in to our
Bunks &c. Saw nor heard Nothing Remarkable
Campaign is no great affliction at present As today Writing
and Drinking Cyder is my Chief imploy.
Jan. 27th
Tuesday.....Behold the Night is past after going the Rounds
with Col. Hathaway & Adjt. Daggett. The Night past in our
traviling the Rounds to all the Guards on the Neck & Drinking
Grogg etc[90].
Cold morning. However had some writing to do.
Wednesday 28th
Moderate weather, However I had considerable writing to do.
I carried off some clothes to be washed &c.
Thursday 29th
Very Rainey Last Night & continueth so this morning. I
turned out in the rain to Notify Officers to Appear after the
Court Martial[91] at Capt. Willmarth's Headquarters.

---

[89]Mathew Randall served as Lieutenant from Hopkington in Captain Thomas Thompson's Company, and as Captain in Col. Joseph Stantons regiment of the Rhode Island Militia.

[90]In spite of private Robinson's casual air, the threat of the British attacking Warwick or Providence remained very real to residents. Governor Nicholas Cooke would write to the President of Congress on January 6, 1778, "The harbour of Newport is filled with the enemy's ships of war, frigates, transports, etc., to the amount of nearly two hundred sail, and we hear that a descent upon the main land is in contemplation by the enemy from Rhode Island".

[91] I have not yet found the official record of this court martial to learn the charges against these men. A clue however, may lie in a penciled page of Carlile's Orderly Book while they were stationed in Pawtuxet for that year, in which is written:

Afternoon I was at Capt. Willmarth's Quarters & saw some of my acquaintences. Returned home and some writing to do &c. Nothing very singular to report to Day onley its Rainey.
Good Night
January 30th 1778
Friday....Pleasant Morning.
Orders come from the Genl. to parade in the afternoon.
Turned out in the morning to the Alarm post and heard the sentence of Bn Bowers[92] & J. Eddy...
Afternoon I was (at) Capt. Willmarth's Quarters. Saw Uncle Metcalf & (?) This afternoon Col. Daggetts Regt. paraded & Genl. Cornell came (and) viewed the Regt. & Exercised them. In the evening Philip returned from home and brought word ye folks were well & likewise brought me two letters – one from EDM & one from (symbol)...I sent two letters home by him.....

"In the whole history of war there is not a single instance of soldiers having taken(,) discharged or converted to their own use the ammunition or implements of war destined for his own defense against the enemy and which they dare (?) secure. The Gen(eral) is sorry to say that the folly and infamy of such conduct was because for the soldiers of Glovers Brigade who have not only in the most villanous manner stolen the ammunition in all the redoubts(,) the (powder?) of the cannon(.) the ladles & plungers & those implements which they ware set to guard but have made it their constant practice to steal as suffer other persons to steal everything that was put under their charge. Ever since they have been stationed here they have now brought.....(unfinished)". (MSS 770, Revolutionary War Papers, Carlile's Orderly Book , Robinson Research Library, Rhode Island Historical Society)
Bowers was not a memeber of Glover's brigade, but the problem seems to have been rampant among troops stationed there and elsewhere during the war.

[92] Bemanuel Bowers of Swansea and Rehobeth, enlisted as a private May 12, 1777 for Lt. Hayes of Capt. Thomas Carlisle's company, Col. Robert Elliot's regiment. Later listed as a gunner in the same company, he officially served until March 16, 1778.. He later enlisted again, but deserted September 2, 1778. (MSSRW, Vol. 2, p. 332)

Saturday 31st

Arose & wrote a letter and Col. Daggett going home. I sent it Mr. E. Da (gge)tt.

Before noon it began to rain and continued a very rainey day however I had considerable writing to do.

Towards night I was at Capt. Willmarth's quarters & in the evening I went in the rain to the Comp. &c. Likewise the cook baked bread in the oven....

The evening past much in jollity & Drinking Cyder.

February 1st 1778

A very Pleasant morning this Sunday may it be a memorable Day to me & a prosperous Life led from it through or Lord & Savior &c.

Wrote some orders and home furloughs &c.

Towards night Capt. Randell came to our quarters and we had a sing…In the evening I went to Adjt. Daggetts quarters(,) from there to one of the Neighbors with the Adjt. & Capt. Randell & Sergt. Mp & Mr. Thurstin where we had a sing with the younger ladys & were treated very generously.

Monday 2nd

Very Pleasant morning So spent the forenoon Chiefly in writing…

Afternoon Colo. Daggetts Regt. paraded for Exercise.

(in the evening made stopples[93] &cc.)

Tuesday 3rd

Pleasant Morning

However a Grand Play and Chores went on in Rising this morning (&Warm Water &cc).

Afternoon paraded for Exercise so we had about two hours on the parade.

In the evening I was at Capt. Willmarth's quarters. Returned home & the evening past in pleasantries…

Feb. 4th Wednesday

---

[93] A plug, or plug with a seal.

Turned out of our bunks as yesterday morning & found a very pleasant morning…

Afternoon ye regt paraded for Exercise..

Toward night Mr. Joseph Daggett[94] came in to our camp & brought word my friend(s) were well. He brought me also a letter from Dr. Bliss with agreeable news.

Nothing more today.

Thursday 5th

Arose & went on to the Alarm post. After breakfast a number of Quakers was at Col. Daggetts quarters & (?) then walked around with J. Daggett. &c.

Afternoon Col. Daggett gave me Furlough so I set off (for) home with J. Daggett.

Traveled as far as Providence & bought us a couple of trinkets the home & cc

Friday 6th

Last Night Mr. J. Daggett tarried with me.

Arose this morning went to Uncle BSR: then to Mrs. Barrows & to see Levy Stanley &ccc[95]. Returned home & got Breakfast, walked around the neighborhood, saw my friends &ccc.

---

[94] Joseph Daggett first enlisted as a private in Capt. Elisha May's company, serving two months in New York from September-November1776. He would later serve in Capt. Israel Trow's company of Col. Josiah whitney's regiment, also with Capt. Stephen Richardson's company in Rhode Island, September-November 1777. During Robinson's time in Warwick he was a civilian, but would re-enlist in July 1778, and is later listed with the men who marched to West Point from Rehobeth in 1780, and served in the 11th Massachusetts Division of the Continental Army. (MSSRW, Vol. 4, P. 351)

[95] Levi Stanley enlisted as a drummer in Capt. Alexander Fosters company of Col. Thomas Carpenter's regiment. Served seventeen days on an expedition to Rhode Island from July 27th through August 12, 1778. Resigned for another twenty-four days on August 17th, serving as a private in Capt. Moses Willmarth's company of Carpenter's regiment through September 9, 1778. (MSSRW, Vol. 14, p. 829)

Towards Night it began to Snow. However I went with Doctor Bliss to Mrs Barrows and got my (supper?) & then went to schoolhouse & sang an hour or two then I set off to Mr. J_ks and Mrs B.

However a very snowy night past.

February 7th
Saturday
Snowy morning however I returned from Mr. J_D.s to E. Daggetts & got Breakfast then he went with me to Dr. Stanley where we stayed an hour or two However I got home about 12 o'clock.

Afternoon was passing Round the Neighborhood &c.

Sunday 8th
It being very snowy walking I stayed at home & did not go to Meeting so I spent some time in reading the Bible.

Towards night I went to Mr. Pullens where I got supper & spent the evening.

Monday 9th
Some snow fall last night However I turned out and went to Mrs. Barrows & Mr. Carpenters then home & got dinner.

Afternoon did some work. In the evening was (at) EDM from thence I went to Mr. JDS…

Tuesday 10th
Returned home & early in ye morning Mother was suddenly (seized) Extremely ill so I hurried after Doc. Man(n). but he was not at home so I returned, she being no better. I went after Doc. Bliss & he was not home so she had no doctor till' in the evening Doctor (?) came however no relief was found so she remained very bad all night.

Feb. 11th Wednesday

Last night I dreamt a frightfull dream. However early in the morning my Father came in to the room & asked if I was a sleep. I answered in the negative. He then told me Mother was not like to live long in his opinion, so I arose & when I saw her face I was persuaded she had not long for this world.

However Doctr. Man(n) came & saw her & he said that there could be no help for her and to our sorrow found it so.

About eleven o'clock she left this world which caused a lamentable day- but the bereaving hand of God comes without delay.

The appointed time is set & no one shall with stand the Mighty Power…it melancholy Day.

Thursday 12th

Last night Mr. ASLS set up with the corpse. Aunt Capron & Mrs Anna (also) tarried at our house.

This morning J. Daggett set off to Warwick to carry my brother the news, however some Snowy in the forenoon.

Preperation is making for the Funeral tomorrow at 1 o'clock.

Went to Mr. Pullens & he came to our house & tarried all night.

XXXIX Hymn 2nd Book pr. D. Watts

1. Our Days alas, our mortal days
   are short & wretched too
   evil and few the Patriarch says
   and well the Patriarch knows

2. Tis but at best a narrow Bound
   that Heav'n allows to men
   and pains & sins run through the Round
   of three score years and ten

3. Well, if ye must be sad and few
   run on my days In hast(e)
   Moments of sin, months of woe
   ye cannot fly to(o) fast.

4. Let heavenly love prepare my soul
   and call her to the skies
   Where years of long salvation call

and glory never dies.

February 13th
Friday…Something Cold…
But behold something more solitary attends the day…
A Day of Weeping is now at hand when the Neighbors &
Friends are gathering together to bury the corpse of my poor
Mother….
This was attended today 1 O'clock
However my brother got home about 12 0'clock today.

Saturday 14th
Very cold. Capt. Read & his wife was at our house this
forenoon then went to D(eaco)n Stanley's and back to Uncle
B(enjamin)S(tanley)R(obinson) and Aunt (?) gave me a peace
of Chees(e) &c.
Nothing Remarkable happened remainder of the day.
Sunday 15th
Pleasant morning so we got breakfast & went to meeting and
heard Mr. Welds preach &ccc.
Returned home & in the evening E. D(agge)tt, G. St(an)ly & R.
St(an)ly were at our house &ccc.
Much might have been learned this day.

Feb. 16th
Monday….This morning some(what)snowy however I got
Breakfast & packd up & then marched to Warwick to join my
Regt. Saw nothing singular in my march however stopped at
Pawtuxet and eat some victuals and drank some cyder.
Then marched on & arrived at Col. Daggetts Quarters about
Sunset. Heard nothing singular in camp…the Col. showed no
displeasure in my staying so long as I did…
Stopt at Mr. Daggetts and Drank with some of my friends.

Tuesday 17th

Pleasant morning as to the sun(')s shining but very cold however I went with Dr. Capron to the Adjt.'s quarters & Drank a morning dram. returned home & eat Breakfast. Heard the ship Warren from Providence went out to sea last night[96].

In the evening the Fray past conferring I Luther at Capt. Warners(?) quarters.

Wednesday 18th

Very pleasant morning however drank a dram with the Mr. Woodcock's.

Afternoon saw JM Hood flog'd &ccc.

Nothing more strange....

February 19, 1778

Thursday...Very pleasant morning so I went on the parade & hears Prayers & saw B. Buffington[97] yok'd & c.

Col. Ha(?) & Doctr Capron & Mr. Wa set off home & Nth Guile[98] came to our quarters.

---

[96] Built in Providence during the British blockade by Sylvester Bowers, the *Warren* was on of the first of thirteen frigates eventually built for the Continental Navy. On 16 February 1778, the ship under command of Capt. John B. Hopkins slipped through the British blockade masked by a snowstorm that in high winds enveloped the harbor in blizzard like conditions. The ship sustained minor damage, but headed to southern waters, and captured two prizes on their way to Bermuda. She had several more successful cruises before her crew was forced to burn her on the Penobscot River in August 1779 to avoid the ship from falling into British hands.

[97] Benjamin Buffington of Rehobeth served three years in Capt. Cole's company. He was reported deserted on March 1, 1778. (MSSRW Vol. 2, p. 767)

[98] Nathan Guile of Preston, enlisted at Worthington, Massachusetts, in the 8th Regiment of Massachusetts, serving seven years and five months until his discharge in 1782. On May 7, 1781, Guile and eighteen other soldiers were placed on trial "for desertion. All but one were found guily and sentenced to "receive one hundred lashes each on their naked backs" (Revolutionary War Records, Orderly Books, National Archives M853, Roll

About sunset my brother returned from home.....
Friday 20th
I arose and went to Capt. Willmarth's quarters then to attend prayers & then home & Breakfast & Mr. Guile set off from our quarters.
Nothing Remarkable happened to Day in Camp in my knowledge.....
Saturday 21st
Cold & windy
In the forenoon was at Capt. Willmarth's quarters.
In the afternoon Adjt. Daggett was at our quarters. Sang some and Suppered...
Sunday 22nd
I arose and went over to Adjt. Daggetts quarters and got some grogg for the Col. so we had a dram this morning...
In the forenoon I went to Meeting and heard Mr. Thatcher preach.
Afternoon I was at a Baptist Meeting at ye Adjt. Quarters.
In the evening some(what) snowy howver I went to Capt. Willmarth's Quarters conferring Allens defecting...[99]

Monday, Feb. 23rd 1778
Doctr Capron returned last evening from home &c[100].

8, p. 36 and MSSRW Vol. 3, p. 69)

[99] Josiah Allen of Attleboro was a private in Capt. Willmarth's company, stationed in Rhode Island where he served 1 month and 28 days of his three-month enlistment. Despite this defection, he later enlisted in Capt. Willmarth's company of Col. Carpenter's regiment August 17th through September 9, 1778, as well as with Capt. Jabez Bullock's company of Carpenter's regiment on the march to Tiverton, and in Capt. Enoch Robinson's company of Dean's regiment July31 to August 8, 1780.(MSSRW, Vol. 1, p. 173)

[100] Comfort Capron enlisted as a surgeon's mate with Col. Timothy Walker's regiment, May 3, 1775. He later served as surgeon in Col. John Daggett's regiment, Brig. General Cornell's brigade, and was stationed in

In the forenoon nothing very strange happened.

Afternoon a flag of truce came up from ye enemy to Warwick Neck with a letter to Gov. Cook[101] & left at night. I sett off (for) Providence and delivered the letter to ye Gov. about eight o'clock and heard him read 'em and found them to be from the Comp. Genl. of the American prisoners concerning them & c[102].

Then I set off again for Warwick and got to Col. Daggetts quarters about 10 o'clock...

However my rice and milk were Cyder & rice.

Tuesday 24th(MSSRW Vol. 3 p. 69)

Warwick, R.I. January 13th- April 1, 1778. He would also serve as a private in Capt. Moses Willmarth's company during its expedition to the state in August of that year, and as Doctor's mate with those detached from the Bristol Co. regiment to reinforce the Continental Army, July 13th to October 31, 1780. MSSRW, Vol. 3, p. 84)

[101] Governor Nicholas Cooke (1717-1782) was the 37th governor of Rhode Island, having served twice as deputy governor, the second time under Governor Joseph Wanton until Wanton was deposed from the post in November 1775 for his Loyalist sympathies. Cooke served as interim governor, and then was elected to his term in 1776, thereby becoming the only governor to have served both colony and independent state. His three years in office were dominated by attending to the concens of war. The occupation of Newport by the British in December 1776 took a heavy toll on the state and the governor, who refused re-election in 1778. He died on September 14, 1782, nearly a year before the signing of the Treaty of Paris. (Arnold, Samuel Greene *History of the State of Rhode Island and Providence Plantations,* Vol. 2, pp. 389-396)

[102] Benjamin Cowell would write that "In the spring of this year (1778), some attempts were made to ameliorate the condition of the prisoners on board the British prison ships in the harbor of Newport; great complaints had been made that the prisoners were not properly treated, that suitable provisions were not made for their accomodations, and moreover, they were half starved; this abuse called up the attention of the Council of war, who empowered Col. Barton 'to proced to Newport, with supplies and necessaries for the prisoners on board the ships, in the jail and hospital at Newport', and that 'he inform himself particularly, of their state, treatment, and wants, and procure and bring an exact list of them". (Cowell, Benjamin *Spirit of '76* p. 163)

Very pleasant morning.

Afternoon I was at Capt W(illmath)'s quarters and saw Mr. Bacon who had lately come (from) Attleboro & brought word the folks were well.

In the evening Col. Hart returned from home.

Wednesday 25th

Exceeding warm & pleasant.

This morning…Col. Carpenter[103] was (at) Col. Dag(getts) Quarters & afternoon Col. Daggets regiment paraded for Exercise.

In the evening was at Adjt's Quart(ers)

Paid bory coat tail (?)

Thursday Feb. 26th

Warm and foggy this morning.

However, Adjt. Daggett set off home (?).Allen, Acknowledgement.

In the forenoon I was at Adjt. Daggetts quarters and saw ye ladyes.

Paraded towards night to Attend prayers etc. In the evening Phillip was at the Col. quart(ers)

NR   I might remark beating the Doct. & J. Daggett playing chess.

Nothing more remarkable this day to Remembrance.

Friday. 27th 1778

This morning some rainey

In the forenoon I was at Ajts Quat(ers) (first wrote J. Bull & T F(?) acknowledgement) in the afternoon.

Nothing Remarkable happened.

---

[103] Colonel Thomas Carpenter was commissioned February 10, 1776 as an officer in the 1st Bristol County regiment. Marched his regiment with eight others to New York under command of Maj. General Lincoln. Was among those who petitioned for a new choice of officers on June 26, 1778. Served in Rhode Island July 24, 1778 through September 11th of that year., also on the alarm at Tiverton, July 26-August 9, 1780 when he ended his service. (MSSRW, Vol. 3, pp. 127-128)

In the evening Snowy, and discourse passed conferring sans(?) money:...

Saturday 28th

This may be a memorable day to J. Allen & Jm Wk, confirming their acknowledgement...

afternoon went a clamming

I was first at the Adjt's quarters after grogg...

March 1, 1778

Sunday...Some orders from the Gen. etc. Went & heard Mr. Thacher preach[104].

However to keep in memory the memorable day the Colonel of Capt. Peck's[105] company me be remark(ing) (viz)

Afternoon, a black fellow[106] came and made his complaint of Corpl Coles[107] striking him.

The Col. ordered him under guard. However the Company ref(used) or a part thereof, and rescued him out which caused a fluster in the Regiment. However the rest of the Company was confined & the prisoner taken up: Lt. Merry[108] is under arrest(?) & Capt. Randall Command(er of the) Guard,

[104] Rev. Peter Thacher was minister of the East Parish of Attleborough from August 1743 until until October 26, 1784, less than a year before his death at the age of seventy. He served as chaplin of Dagget's regiment at the time of Robinson's service.(Daggett, Sketch of the history of Attleborough, p. 63)

[105] Capt. Peleg Peck served in the 4th Company of the Swansey Militia under Col. Thomas Carpenter's regiment. He was stationed in both Warwick and Tiverton during the year the incident occurred. He would sign a petition with others in June 1778 asking for a new choice of officers. (MSSRW, Vol. 12, p. 53)

[106] I have identified at least eight individuals within Peck's company who were men of color. They are, in alphabetical order, Charles Aarpia, of black and indigenous origin, Prince Barney of Swansea, Wheaton Barney, Dan Brown, James Hall, James Hill, Claber Tarbot, and Scipio Thomas.

[107] Likely Corporal Isaiah Cole (1731-1810) of Swansea who was first enrolled in the Massachusetts Militia on December 29, 1777. (MSSRW, Vol. 3, p. 765)

Monday 2nd

Last night & this morning snowy. However the prisoners were all brought before the Gen(eral) and Colonels and those that went to rescue the boy out were all confined & the two Corp(orals) put in irons. Those that pled ignorant in the affair were dismissed from under guard.

(Tues) It was found out that Capt. Peck had some of his Brothers to Suttle out & the Genl. gave orders for Col. Daggett to sease the same, and (re)turn it to the store which was accordingly performed…

I went & saw the prisoners

(saw Betsey & Nancy)

Carried my Cloathes to the water…

March 3, 1778 Tuesday,

Morning Snowy, the Colonels were at the General's & had the prisoners in examination. Orders came from Gen(eral) Spencer[109] Confirming ye prisoners, etc.

This day is called pancake day[110] by ye inhabitants of this place and kept in memory by eating on (this) day. However in ye forenoon I had just a taste of ye…

---

[108] Timothy Merrey of Swansea, served as 1st Lieutenant in Peck's Company. (MSSRW, Vol. 10, p. 635)

[109] Joseph Spencer was an attoeney from East Haddam, Connecticut. At the outbreak of the American Revolution he was a Brigadier-General of the Connecticut Militia, and led them as the 1st Connecticut Regiment to support the Seige of Boston in April 1775. When the 1st Regiment was adopted into the Continental Army, he retained his rank, and was appointed Major General in 1776. He would take part in the Campaign on Rhode Island under Sullivan, but would resign his commission on June 14, 1778 after a Congressional inquiry into his cancelling a planned attack on Aquidneck Island. (Whittelsey, Charles Barney, *Historical Sketch of Joseph Spencer* Sons of the American Revolution, Connecticut, 1996)

Towards night I was at the Adjt's quarters where there were a number of ladys and I had a fine supper of pcakes etc.

Adjt. Daggett returned from home & brought a letter from C. Stanley

Snowy evening.

Wednesday 4th

...It cleared of snowing this morning. In the forenoon of ye day kept pretty close to my quarters.

Afternoon the Regiment paraded and the prisoners were brought before the regiment & General Cornell's orders were that the prisoners be discharged from further confinement & their handcuffs be taken off. This was accordingly performed. After this we had a sing etc.

Thursday 5th

Pleasant morning etc.

In the forenoon I was at Adjt. Daggetts quarters.

afternoon Col. Daggetts Regt. paraded for exercise, meanwhile I did some writing.

(Col. Hathaway's son came to see 'em)

March 6, 1778

Friday

Pleasant morning...

However I went early in ye morning to E(lijah) Warners and eat a very good Breakfast at ye (Eligs)

Returned back and a detached party from Capt. Hick's company were sent to Rumstick Neck[111].

---

[110] Traditionally associated with Shrove Tuesday, griddlecakes were served as part of the feasting, and using of the last of the winter's perishible provisions before Lent. In Rhode Island, the traditional pancakes came from Maize introduced by the indigenous people and were commonly called johnnycakes.

[111] Rumstick Neck is the southernmost point of Barrington, a penisula whose western beach faces Narragansett Bay, and whose eastern side flanks a cove between Rumstick and Adams Point, at the entrance to the Warren River.

Captain Dagget and Capt. Willmarth went up to the Fulling Mill.

Afternoon regiment paraded for exercise.

In the evening I was at ye Adjt's quarters the (fray?) past concerning Sgt Major Lincoln[112] etc.

Saturday 7th 1778

Some snowy. However Phillip was at our quarters.

Afternoon I went to the Adjt's quarters and got my cloathes. returning back, saw the Rev. Mr. Welds who had come down to preach with ye soldiers., and brought news Uncle Thomas Daggett was dead[113].

In the evening Adjt. Dagget & QM was at our quarters & we had some singing.

Some news was told concerning the murder at Brookfield & the officers deserting to R(hode) Island[114].

---

[112]Asa Lincoln enlisted January 29, 1778 and served as Sergeant Major in Col. John Dagget's regiment through April 1st. He then signed on for three months in Rhode Island under Brigadeer General Ezekial Cornell. The fray in which he was involved is unclear. (MSSRW Vol. 9, p. 800)

[113] Thomas Daggett was born on the island of Martha's Vineyard in 1688. He was the son of John Daggett and Sarah Norton/Pease. He was the brother of Robinson's grandmother Patience Daggett Robinson. He died in the 90th year of his age in Attleborugh on March 6, 1778.

[114] Robinson refers to the murder of Joshua Spooner, a prominent Brookfield farmer by his wife Bathsheba Ruggles Spooner, daughter of Brigadier General Timothy Ruggles of Worchester, Massachusetts. The Spooners had been married for eleven years and had four children by the spring of 1777, when a sixteen year old soldier named Ezra Ross fell ill on his way home to Ipswich, and was invited into the spooner home, where Bathsheba nursed him back to health. The soldier visited the home several more times during furloughs from duty that year and befriended the husband, often accompanying him on business trips. But by December 1777, Ross and Bathsheba were in the throes of an affair, with Ross staying over the holiday into the New Year. By January, Mrs. Spooner confronted her lover with the news that she was pregnant, and encouraged him in several methods of disposing of her husband. The next month, when Ross accompanied Spooner on another trip, he brought along a bottle of nitric acid, provided by Bathsheba, to poison her husband. In the

Nothing more remarkable happened in my knowledge (this day)

Sunday ye 8th March

Slipery walking....However in the forenoon I went & heard Mr. Weld preach.

Returned back at noon & Mr. Weld dined in the Col's....Afternoon I went to meeting again & heard a very good sermon & very suitable for the time,

After meeting Mr. Weld supped with the Col(onel).

In the evening I was at Capt. Willmarth's quarters with J. Daggett & see the news Print I found we had drawed the value of one ticket in the lottery at Providence.

Returned home to my quarters and bundled to bed.

Monday 9th

I arose & went & led Mr. Weld his horse (?) Returned back (from) Mr. Weld(')s went to prayers in the Col. quarters then went to Breakfast with the Col. After this was performed he sett off home...

(Parole- Weld (?) sign Thatcher)

---

end, Ross lacked the nerve to commit murder and returned home.

Bathsheba Ruggles must have suspected that her lover lacked the nerve, and while the men were away, encountered two British runaways-one Seargent James Buchanan, and Pvt. William Brooks, and invited them into her home; and the plot to kill her husband. The pair willingly obliged, and Brooks killed Mr. Spooner as he returned from a nearby tavern. Summoned by Bathsheba, Ezra Ross helped Buchanan to hide the body of Mr. Spooner in a well. Bathsheba paid the men with money from her husband's lockbox, and gave them a horse to ride to Worcester. Brooks and Buchanan drank the night away in a tavern, where the paper money the men used to pay for drinks and the shiny shoe buckles on Brooks worn boots drew attention. Once word of the murder arrived from Brookfield, just fourteen miles away, the three men were quickly arrested and revealed the tale of Bathseba Spooner's plots of homicide. The three men and Bathsheba Spooner, who had pled for leniency for her unborn child, were hung before a crowd of five-thousand spectators on July 2, 1778 in Worcester's Washington Square.

In the afternoon I went with ye Adjt. & Sgt. Major to Capt. Nichols quarters-perform some jollity...

Returned back & in the evening E(nsign?) Warner was at the Col's quarters. Com(?) Stelle[115] brought some orders from Providence (,) which I had to record, concerning rations, etc.

March 10, 1778

Tuesday... Snowy morning...

Major Slade set off (for) home very early in the morning...

I went with Doctr Capron to ye Adjt. quarters & drank a dram. Returned back & did some writing then went to Capt. Willmarths quarters. Came back and cut my finger which caused me trouble...

Afternoon I was at the Adjt's quarters & Col. Daggett set off for Providence.

In the evening we had some grogg...the Col. returned about 8 o'clock...

Wednesday 11th

Arose and drank a glass of grogg & spent some time in writing, etc. Got Breakfast and went over to Adjt's quarters and found muddy walking & some rainey.

Afternoon I was at Capt. Willmarth's quarters. Towards night Mr. John Woodcock[116] came in to camp.

Thursday 12th 1778

Arose & got Breakfast and went to E(nsign) Warner(')s Returned back & Col. Hathaway went to OpD Newtown...

---

[115] Likely Benjamin Stelle who served as Adjunct of Richmonds and Major BenjaminTallman's company of ther Rhode Island regiments from November 1775 through 1777, and as paymaster from 1 June 1779 to 1st April 1781.

[116] John Woodcock of Attlebouro first enlisted as a private in Capt. Stephen Richardson's company of mintemen who answered the alarm of April 19, 1775, and also served at Bunker Hill. His name is on Capt. Richardson's list of the men who signed on for the "Grand Campaign of all" aor three years service. He would sunsequently serve as corporal in Capt. Moses Willmarth's Company of Daggetts regiment, and Sergeant in Capt. Alexander Foster's company of Dean's regiment. (MSSRW, Vol. 17, pp. 822-823)

Mr. Richardson home , Baris (?) home, Capt. Randall & Company move to Providence- Capt. Robinson came in camp….

Friday March 13, 1778
Very warm morning hoever we had a barrel of Cyder brought in to quarters… from yesterday I have been some(what) unwell with a bad cold…
In the forenoon I went in to Mr. Lippits room & conversed with ye young ladys ..
Afternoon ye Col(onel) & staff officers and waiters[117] went a Clamming and I was left alone.
Nothing more remarkable happened…
The word passed well…
Saturday 14th
Very warm weather.
Colonel Daggett went over to Lt. Brintnell's[118] detachment before noon. M. Master Kingsbury came to muster of regiment. However we had _____ for dinner and then the business proceeded in mustering the men…
Col. Hathaway returned from UP. Newtown…In the evening had the Whisler to carry on ye joke…
March 15th 1778

---

[117] Waiters or orderlys, as they were also called, were the black slaves assigned to officers of the regiment. Such service often earned them their freedom, but not always. Rhode Island would offer its slaves that opportunity for a short time, after an Act by the General Assembly in February 1778 approved a recruitment plan by General James Mitchell Varnum to form a regiment made entirely of slaves from the state. However many of those already in the service of an officer remained in their positions, and rarely took up arms.

[118] Lt. Ebenezer Brintnell was commissioned on 21 March 1776 as 1st. Lieutenant in Capt. Samuel White's 7th company of Daggetts regiment. At the time of Robinson's mention of a "fray", he was likely visiting his son Obidiah, who was then a private with Capt. Israel Trow's company, stationed with the other Massachusetts men in Rhode Island. (MSSRW, Vol. 2, p. 547)

Sunday…Very pleasant however some business passed concerning the muster roll.

Was at the Genl's quarters then to meeting & heard Mr. Thatcher…

At noon I was at the Capt. quarters, afternoon was at meeting. In the evening I was at Capt. Willmarth's quarters…Returned home & got some supper & bundled in…nothing more at present.

Wednesday 16th

Some Rainey thru day However I wrote some furloughs. J. Dagget & Wood(coc)k set off for home. Towards noon I was at Capt. Willmarth's Quarters, and E. Bacon came to camp so we passed some conversations & he went home with me & then to ye Adjt's quarters about 12 o'clock he went home…

Afternoon I went into Mrs Lippits Room & saw the ladys[119]. Col. Dagget yesterday & today very poor.

17th March 1778

Lousy morning However paraded for parayers and ye Sergt. Major s(ai)d the Psalm, etc.

Returned back and saw Capt. Wilmarth who had been the Rounds last night. The Colonel remain(s) some(what) unwell. Lt. Tylers party returned from ye Fulling Mill &c.

Afternoon I went to Judge Lippits and drank coffee and see the Ladys & in the evening was at Captain Wilmarths.

18th March 1778

Very Pleasant morning. &c.

In the forenoon I was at ye Adjt's quarters & then to Capt. Wilmarths.

Returned home and got dinner & then went to the Gen(era)l.

---

[119] Mrs. Welthyan Greene Lippit, was the wife of longtime town clerk Jeremiah Lippit, whose large colonial house lay along the Shore Road just above the entrance to Warwick Neck. The ladies may well have been her daughters, Ann Lippit, who was married to Col. Christopher Greene, Elizabeth Lippit. amd Welthian Lippit, who had married William Greene in 1774.(Fuller, Oliver Payson, The History of Warwick, Rhode Island)

Returned back and found the Field & Staff Officers exercising & then the Regiment paraded for Exercise.

In the evening I went in to Mrs Lippit's room---the American bhalling---Mrs Betsey[120].

March 19, 1778

Fine and Pleasant Day

The forepart of the day not much past only that I was at Capt. Wilmarth's quarters and found my brother had the measles and a number more of his Company…[121]

Afternoon the Regt. paraded (for) exercise.

Mr. Draper came in to camp…in the evening I was at the Adjt's Quarters and drank Egg-Pop[122], Returned and then went to the Guard house.

Friday 20th March 1778

Arose before the firing of the gun and went with Lt. Col. Hathaway to the Guard House and took a pack of cards Returned back & it being a very pleasant day Col. Daggett set off for home about 10 o'clock & then I took a walk with Doctor Capron.

---

[120]Perhaps the woman Robinson refers to earlier as "Black Bettey". Women often followed soldiers from place to place under an umbrella of consent for the morale of the troops. I make this assumption based upon his portrayal as "the American Bhalling" a woman of foreign origin. This also raises the possibility that the woman was a servant of Mrs Lippit, and not the same woman, as the journal later rferences having tea with Mrs Lippit and Mrs Betsey".

[121] The disease affected a number of men that winter. The "Weekly Return of the Sick in Col. Daggett's Regiment" dated February 12, 1778 and submitted by Comfort Capron, lists seven men whose bout with the disease left them temporarily "unfit for dute". Two weeks later, the number was down to four.

[122] A version of eggnog-nog, meaning a drink that was generally a mix of egg, rum, and sugar. A tourist noted the habit of American travelers taking a draught of egg-nog before a long journey. The same was true of soldiers before a long watch. (see Weld, Isaac Jr. *Travels Through the States of North America and the Provinces of Upper and Lower Canada during the years 1795, 1796, and 1797* London, John Stockdale, 1800 Vol. 1, p. 98)

Returned home I found two Hessian Gentlemen up on their parole to go into Rhode Island.

In the evning I was in Mrs Lippits Room & saw ye Ladys & J. Daggett & JW(?) returned from home &c.

Saturday 21st March 1778

Very Windy & Cold

However Mr. Thatcher went to prayers in the Guard House

Then I went to Capt. Wilmarth's quarters and saw my brother who remains unwell with the measles &c.

Returned home and went to the Adjt's quarters

Afternoon ye Col. May went up to Capt. Garzeas quarters so we had the room to ourselves and played checkers.

Sunday 22 March 1778

Last night I bundled in with the Doctr. Arose & a very cold morning we found

However I went to the Adjt's with the doctor and drank a morning dram. The two Hessian Gentlemen set off for Rhode Island.

In the forenoon I went and heard Mr. Thatcher preach

Afternoon to meeting again with Mrs N_____ Lpt.

Saw my brother at noon &c.

In the evening was in Mrs Lippits room –The Major jollity…

Further I might remark (on) this day as it Brings me to the 20(th)

year of age…..

Monday 23, March

Arose and went to the Guard House & attended prayers-then went to Capt. Wilmarth's quarters and saw my brother who has the measles coming out very well.

The Major set off up to the fulling mill &c.

Then we played Ball[123] & after that drank Grogg &c.

---

[123] While Abner Doubleday is credited with inventing baseball in 1839, many sources point to variations of the game being played long before, and especially among soldiers of the Revolutionary War. Historian Thomas L. Altheer, published pages from the journal of Officer Henry Dearborne of

Towards night attended prayers again
Nothing remarkable more happened
Col. Tyler[124] dined with ye Colonel.
Tuesday 24th
Very pleasant day so I arose & attended prayers & went to
Capt. Willmarths quarters.
Returned home (The Gam Bt Lt) and then a sing past the
forenoon
Corporel Supur(?) dined with us & Col. Tylor with Col.
Hathaway
About sunset Col. Daggett and Mr. Woodcock returned from
(home).
Nothing more remarkable
March 25, 1778
Wednesday   Very cold and lousy. I attended prayers and
then went and saw my brother.
Returned and got Breakfast and went up to John Worners(,)
Ensign D.T. A.L.M. General (/)
Towards night paraded for prayers & in the evening I went
with Doctr Capron and saw Mr. Barrows who was very sick[125].
Tarried about an hour and returned...
In the forenoon wey'd provisions.

---

a New Hampshire regiment that records an episode on April 3, 1779 when "all the officers of the Brigade came out and play'd a game at ball the first we have had this yeare", and on April 17th, "we are oblige'd to walk 4 miles to day to find a place leavel enough to play ball". Baseball historians point to a number of games which include a bat, ball, and running to a post or bases that existed in colonial times. It is worth noting also, that Doubleday himself was a veteran.

[124] Ebenezer Tyler served as Sergeant in Capt. Jacob Ides company of the Attleboro militia, as 1st Lieutenant in Capt. Samuel Robinson's 4th Bristol Company, and as Lieutenant in Capt. Moses Wilmarth's company. At the time of Robinson's journal, he had enlisted in that capacity for 2 months and 29 days in Rhode Island. (MSSRW, Vol. 16, p. 231)

[125] This seems to be David Barrows, who enlisted in Capt. Wills Company of Daggett's regiment at Bristol, Rhode Island, 1776-1777. (MSSRW, Vol. 1, p. 697)

Thursday 26th 1778

Lousy and cold morning.

However attended prayers and Jonathan Woodcock set off after Doctr weeks for Mr. Barrows & afternoon drank tea with Mrs. Lippit & Mrs. Betsey

Towards night it snowed and Mr. Aaron & William Barrows came down to carry their brother home..[126]

Nothing remarkable happened only Mrs. Higgins going on to Rhode Island.

Friday 27th 1778

Lousy and some snow in the morning…

However the Mr Barrows set off for home with their brother This day my business passed chiefly in settling the Officers extreonary Ration of the Col. Mess.

Saturday 28th

Business past in deciding provisions etc.

Afternoon the (?) past with the Sergt. Major concerning coats. Towards night ye Regt. paraded for exercise.

In the evening Capt Randall came from Providence with a letter requesting Col. Daggetts regiment to Tarry fifteen days from 1st of April.

March 29th 1778

Sunday- Arose and went to the Adjt's and drank a dram. Col. Daggetts Regt. paraded and heard the request of last nights letter &c.

However none paid but all ordered to return home.

[126] Aaron and William Barrows were brothers to the deceased David Barrows. All three were the sons of Benejah and Priscilla Philbrook Barrows. Both brothers would also serve during the war, Aaaron as 2nd Lietenant in Col. Thomas Carpenter's regiment, sent into Rhode Island 17 August 1778, and serving until 19 September. William enlisted as a private in Capt. Jabez Ellis' company, as well as with Capt. Jacob Ide's company of Daggetts regiment which marched to Rhode Island 8 December 1776. He would serve with Capt. Stephen Richardson's company of Col. George Williams regiment on a secret expedition to the state 25 September 1777. He would return to Rhode Island the following year with Capt. Elisha May's company of Daggetts regiment, serving from 23 August 1778 through 2 September 1778 when he was discharged. (MSSRW, Vol. 1, pp. 665, 702)

Heard Mr. Townson preach fore & afternoon

In the evning I went to the Adjt's and saw the ladys &c.

Monday 30th 1778

Lasst night and this morning very stormy, however I went with the doctor and drank a morning dram.

In the forenoon I wrote considerably, thus the major part of the day past

Towards night proof read for more (proposals?) in the evening to settle our Mess reckoning however by reason of dispute got but little way in the business.

Evening past with XX's & with the Colonel.

March 31, 1778

Tuesday…Lousy weather, however in the morning the Sergt. Major & Quarter Master Sergt. (Pain?) & Perrium come to get the Col. to sign their Warrant which was not done however they made sour punch very free.

Orders to return in our cartridges and march to Providence Business enough.

Wednesday April 1st 1778

This memorable day being come about we arose very early and packed up & got Breakfast (then the fray) Past with the Major & his pipe and about eight o'clock we left Old Warwick & ye kind inhabitants and marched for home (Mr. Sallm. Read bringing our pack and to be short- arrived at home about Day light down and to my great satisfaction found them well excepting my father who had a swelling on his throat…

April 2nd 1778

In the forenoon I was at Adjt. Daggetts

Afternoon I went to Town Meeting (concerning the new laws &C.) at night I went with Mr. Joel Read

In the evening Capt. Read & Aunt came home some(what) hurt by being turned over in their Chairs

Tarried all night

Friday 3rd

Arose and got Breakfast and Mr. J. Read came home with me.
Afternoon I had a sing at the schoolhouse
At night I went with E. Daggett and got supper & then ....
Saturday 4th
Very Pleasant Day. Returned home.

Notes on back pages:
Friends Mis(s) Friends
Stand Bearing your disposition,
A man _____ the world
is Contempt while the Ambitious
ridicule when married XXX &c.
A True Coppy Examined

Field Officers for Col. Daggets Regt.
John Daggett   Col.
John Hathaway Lt. Col.
Peleg Slade Major
Staff
Adj. Daggett
Q. Master French
Surgeon Capron
Chaplain Thatcher
NR: The chaplain ranks before the Adjt. alltho I have set the
Adjt first in the catalogue.
Asa Lincoln Sergt. Major
Joseph Daggett Quarter Master sergeant
Noah Robinson Junior, clerk to Col. Daggetts,
Gen. Cornells Brigade, Warwick

The Lippit Homestead, circa 1720. Courtesy of the Warwick Historical Society

"stopped at Pawtuxet and eat some victuals and drank some cyder" The Carder Tavern, circa 1756

Volume III. Noah Robinson's Book, Swansey ...1778

Money received for my Following Campaign:
July 24[127] Received of Deacon Jnth. Stanley[127]   14L 12S
as a bounty and Twilings Tea
Sept. 21st Received of Lt. Enoch Robinson   9L 0S
AM as additional pay from Capt. May's Campaign
Nov. 25th Received of Capt. May   15L
Dec. 15th Received of Capt. Cole   5L 14S

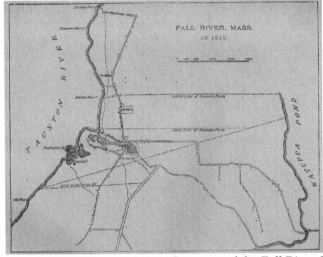

Later map of Fall River, dated1812. Courtesy of the Fall River Historical Society

---

[127] Jonathan Stanley (1733-1811) was the younger brother of Deborah Stanley Robinson, Noah's mother. They shared another younger brother, named Soloman (1740-1819). On this occasion, Robinson's forty-five year old uncle was paying him to serve in his stead. (Find A Grave Memorial # 43882260).

Journal of a Six Month Campaign by God's Permition in the State of R. Island in a Company Commanded by Capt. Caleb Richardson...from the town of Attleboro...

Boys to Play
The horn does blow for us to go
And fight our Enemies
We'll take our guns & swing our packs
and Never turn our Backs
In God we Trust
and Fear em' not
Brave Sullivan's[128]
to Lead us on

---

[128] General John Sullivan was the third son of an Irish schoolmaster in Somersworth, New Hampshire. Sullivan was well educated and studied law between 1758-1760, opening up his own practice in Berwick, Maine in 1763, before moving back to New Hampshire to practice law the following year. He built a friendship with Royal Governor John Wentworth, and was appointed a Major in the local militia in November 1772. The effects of the Boston Tea Party caused a seperation between the two men. Nonetheless, Sullivan was appointed to a seat in the Continental Congress.

In Philadelphia, Sullivan would be appointed brigadier-general in the Continental Army, and leave that city to take part in the Seige of Boston. He was later sent to Quebec, to rally the dispirited and defeated troops there, then to Long Island, where he took part in the futile attempt to stem the British tide reaching New York. He was captured, but released in time to rejoin Washington before the Battle of Trenton where his division secured a key bridge over the Assunkpick Creek, cutting off an escape route for the Hessian soldiers. He would later lead troops with mixed success in the Battles of Princeton, Brandywine, and Germantown. In early 1778 he was assigned to Rhode Island as Commander of the Continental troops and combined militia amid plans to take back the British occupied Island of Acquidneck. (Whitmore, Charles P. *A General of the Revolution: John Sullivan of New Hampshire* New York, Columbia University Press 1961 and Golway, Terry *Washington's General: Nathanael Greene and the Triumph of the American Revolution* Owl Books 2006 p. 91)

July 20, 1778

This morning Began my Days work with J. Pullen however worked about twenty-five minutes and engaged in the Six Month Campaign with R. St(anle)y (for Capt. May) so we left our business & went to Capt. Richardson's however returned without seeing the Capt.

Tuesday 21st
Arose and got Breakfast and then went with my Mates to Taunton & past muster-saw Capt. Richardson & got leave to tarry at home until Saturday next. Returned home & in the evening was at ye W. (?) tarried with M (?)

Wednesday 22nd July 1778
Helped my father Reap his rye.

Thursday 23rd.
Rode Round the neighborhood with Doctor Bliss, E. Daggett, E. B(acon) & Betsey and saw my friends…

Friday 24th 1778
Was at the Wd. St(anley)'s & bought some Grogg.

Saturday 25th
Marched from home in company with G. Stanley, R. Stanley, & O.B. to Brown's Tavern in Swansey where we joined Capt. Richardson's Company.

Sunday 26th
Nothing Material happened
so stay(ed) at Browns.
In the evening The Capt. put me in as a clerke.

Monday 27th July 1778

Marched from Brown's & crossed the ferry and took barraks at Bardin's about a mile and a half from ye ferry and got Boarded at Churches[129].

Tuesday 28th

In the forenoon went on fatigue & cut fashends. Afternoon did some Writing at Doc. Turners.

Wednesday 29th

Heard there was a company of soldiers from Attleboro at Brown's…at night was at Bardin's & drank Grogg.

Thursday 30th

Was at Slade(s) ferry[130] and saw Capt. Stephen's company-heard from home & then went by water to Brown's after provisions[131]. Returned & saw Capt. Stephen's company.

Friday 31st July

Got Breakfast and went to Capt. Stephen's company. Went down to ye ferry & washed etc. Returned home & had two large puddings for dinner.

Heard Uncle E. Robinson was recovering his health.

---

[129] The ferry lay at the northwesternmost point of Fall River. Though there was a footpath along the Taunton River, the regiment would likely have walked west on Ferry Lane until it met North Main Street, and then headed south towards Deacon's Point and the intersection of Bedford Street before encamping on the farmlands east of the coastline.

[130] Slade's Ferry was named for William Slade, a large landowner whose holdings included the ferry landing along the Taunton River, just south of where the Brightman St. Bridge is located. The ferry would be run by the family until the river was bridged in 1876. At the time of the war, the family also seems to have run their house as a tavern or inn, which the soldiers frequented. (Wright, *History of Swansea 1667-1917*, Swansea, 1917, pp. 176-177, and Rose, Constance M., *Swansea in the War of the Revolution,* from the *Swansea Stagecoach,* Swansea Historical Society, 1976) p. 30

[131] Brown's Tavern was located in Dighton, Massachusetts located at the beginning of the tidewater of the Taunton River. At the time of the Revolution, it was a shipbuilding community. The journey by water would have been about six miles.

By Movement it appeared that there would be a Defense made in R. Island in a short time…

Sat. 1st August 1778
Went on fatigue and cut tent poles then returned to Bardins and drank fatigue Rum very plentifully[132] (&) by that means returned to churches very happy-towards night I was at Capt. Stephen's company and saw the dance & jollity carried on by the officers, etc.

Sunday 2nd
Saw Mr. Whittiker then went up to Capt. Stephen's Company when Capt. Sa(muel) R(ichard)son passed by with a company from Attleboro. Saw Lt. E. Rob(inso)n and many of my acquaintances. Heard the folks were well at home…
Monday 3rd August 1778
In the forenoon was at Capt. Stephen's Company. Saw J. Daggett at town then returned to Churches where they dined with us.
In the evening sang P(iano) tunes and heard the ladys sing songs…
Tuesday 4th
Afternoon I was at Capt. Stephen's company with R. Stanley.
Wednesday 5th
Heard one of the Enemies ships was blown up. Did some Writing etc.
Capt. Richardson went out of camp…
Towards Night heard two more British ships were blown up[133].

---

[132] It was a longstanding military tradition in British, and thus, Americanized forces to rely upon rum as a stimulant to induce labor, or a late march from the troops; often called "fatigue duty". (see David T. Courtwright *Forces of Habit: Drugs and the Making of the Modern World* Harvard University Press, 2001)

[133] Robinson refers to the results of action taken by the French captain of the *Fantasque*, who, after reconnetiring the waters off Conanicut Island, spied with his glass four British frigates to the north of the island, and a fifth

Thursday 6th August 1778

Drew seven day provisions. Was at Capt. Stephen's Company etc.

In the evening saw Lt. Robinson then had some singing at Churches with ye Ladys.

Friday 7th

Gen. Varnum's & Gen. Glovers brigade, Col. Jackson & Col Shearburne's Regt. of Continental troops crossed the ferry...I saw some of my acquaintances among the troops...

Saturday 8th

Arose and drank egg Rum & eat Breakfast –about Twelve o'clock marched on through heat and dust to Howland's Ferry and encamped on the ground.

Heard some firing towards Newport.

Sunday 9th August

Arose and went to ye Grogg shop & drank a dram & about seven o'clock three deserters came of R. Island...several more soon followed them.

---

in the harbor. Seeking to takeadvantage of the temporary naval superiority, he requested permission to attack the frigates, and Admiral d'Estaing agreed, adding a third double decker to Pierre-André de Suffren's arsenal, the Protectur; which carried 64 guns, the same as the Fantasque, along with the Sagittaie, a fifty gun ship under command of Captain d'Abert de Rions. The British were aware that they were spied upon, and orders were sent to the frigates captains that under no circumstances were they to allow their ships to be captured. On August 5th the French gunners approached the channel, and strove to cut off the British frigates, the Cerebus, the Juno, the Lark, and the Orpheus from Newport harbor. Under heavy fire, the captain of the Cerebus ran her aground, had the crew cut her masts, and set her ablaze. The other French captains then took similar action, with Captain Charles Hudson driving the Orpheus ashore on Coggeshall Point, and setting it on fire, and Captain Richard Smith of the HMS Lark finding himself trapped between Arnold and Coggeshall Point, doing the same. The galley Pigot would also be set afire, and the Juno would hold out the longest, before the crew raced in longboats to the shore by the light of the blaze. (McBurney, Christian, "*The Rhode Island Campaign: The First French and American Operation in the Revolutionary War,* PA, Westholme, 2011 pp 89-92)

About eight o'clock pack up, took boat & crossed Howland Ferry on to R. Island.

Formed and marched boldly up to the Fourts on the N. end of ye island then was informed ye enemy had retreated to the (?) end of ye island so we lay on our post until about four o'clock when a shower came up so that we got very wet...[134]

At night bundled down as last night- some rain fell so that we got wet,,,

Monday 10th August 1778

Last night encamped on our post with our blankets, Rainey and we got very wet. Lousy this morning.

Much firing below ye island[135].

Wrote a letter home &c.

Tuesday 11th

Lousy morning. Saw Mr. Whittaker & Pitcher[136] and many others from Attleboro.

---

[134] The British made several attempts to kidnap mainlanders for interrogation of what they knew of American plans. When they did succeed, they were given false information- that Gen. Benedict Arnold was aboard one of the French vessels with a contingent of Contnental troops to invade the Island. Believing this news, British Commander Robert Pigot ordered the troops to abandon the redoubt on the southern end of Aquidneck Island, and pull back to the city of Newport.(McBurney, p.93)

[135] Around 8:30 am that morning, the French fleet had sailed within range of Pigot's batteries on the island. The resulting exchange of cannon fire caused much destruction, both to the town, which suffered hits from the French fire which often overshot the fortifications, as well as to the French themselves, whose dead washed ashore on the beaches of Rhode Island. (Deardon, Paul F. *The Seige of Newport: Inauspicious Dawn of Alliance* from *Rhode Island History, Jan.-April 1970,* Providence, Rhode Island Historical Society, 1970 pp. 22-23

[136] Oliver Whitaker of Attleboro was a private in Capt. Elisha May's company of Daggett's regiment. He would serve eleven days in Rhode Island in September 1778. (MSSRW Vol. 17, p. 23) Jabez Pitcher of Attleboro enlisted as a private with Capt. Jabez Ellis' company of minutemen and marched on the alarm of April 19, 1775 for eleven days, later served with Capt. Stephen Richardson's company, which marched September 25, 1777, and served for 1 month and six days. He was also among those who marched on a secret expedition under command of Col.

About 11 o'clock had orders to be ready to march by b4 o'clock-at 4 o'clock the whole army paraded and was viewed by the Chief General-general orders to reddy to march by six o'clock tomorrow for N. Port. Drew a tent & packed...

Wednesday 12th August 1778

Last night very stormy However was very happy thinking we had a tent-turned out & baked Bannak and boiled rice.

It being very stormy we did not perform last night's orders so we kept our camp & drank grogg.

Thursday 13th

Last night windy and stormy so that our tent blew up and caused us much trouble getting very wet[137].

Turned out & eat raw jerky & Bannock. Drank Rum & boiled rice.

A great storm susseaded & heard there was eleven deserters came of last night to our Army.

Nothing further remarkable.

Friday 14th August 1778

Last night the storm abated.

About 4 o'clock was mustered and had orders to pack(?) our provisions and clean our Arms without delay.

Genl. orders for the Army to move to N.Port by six o'clock tomorrow morning.

Saturday 15th 1778

George Williams, and would later serve with Capt. Alexander Foster's company of Carpenter's regiment for seven days in Tiverton, Rhode Island, before being discharged on July 27, 1780. (MSSRW Vol. 12, p. 443)

[137] Historian Samuel Greene Arnold would write of the storm's effect upon the troops: "...The tents were prostrated, and the army, exposed on the wet ground to a cold and drenching rain, suffered severely. Some of the men died from exposure, and a great number of horses perished. The ammunition was much damaged, some of it entirely spoiled..." (Arnold, Samuel Greene, *History of the State of Rhode Island and Providence Plantations* New York, Appleton & Co. 1860) Vol. 2, p. 423

Turned out by times and packed up at six o'clock a signal was fired and the whole Army paraded in a vigilant posture then a signal was fired and ye Army moved-marched with great spirit about 4 miles and halted about an hour or two then marched on as before within about two miles and a half of Newport town-pitched tents-in ye evening was (?) out...[138]

Sunday 16th August 1778
Lousy morning, however turned out at ye beat of ye revellee. Had coffee and junk for Breakfast.
Was at Capt. Robinson's company & received a letter from J. Read.
Since last night our men have been very delinquent in trench making[139].
Towards night four men from Easton joined Capt. Richardson's company.

---

[138] At 7:00 am, three successive booms of cannon sent the signal for some 11, 895 men to commence the march on Newport. Colonel Henry Beekman Livingston's advance guard led the march south, about a mile ahead of the remaining troops. Pioneer units armed with axes, shovels and hoes followed to help clear the roads as the remainder of the army, and cannons followed. Dividing into three columns, Varnums' Brigade headed down the West Road, General's Greene and Cornell's Brigades filed down the center, and Glover's Brigade marched along the East Road. Major General John Hancock's Massachusetts militia tramped behind Greene and Cornell's troops, with two reserve regiments of Rhode Island militia behind, under command of Brigadier General William West. Colonel John Crane's artillery units pulled two heavy cannons down the East Road and two more along the West Road, while detachments from Connecticut and other militia covered the flanks. (MCBurney p. 139)

[139] Just before sunset on August 16th, some 800 men were given the task of digging trenches for the upcoming assault. 400 men dug trenches in which a four cannon battery would be placed just north of Green End road, and under a mile from British defenses. Another 400 men dug a "covered way" or concealed trench, from the first battery, down the westward slope of Honeyman Hill to the first of a series of American batteries. Through the night and into a fog -shrouded morning, the men piled earthworks buttressed with facines to face the British lines. (McBurney, pp. 143-144)

Some Cannonading from the Enemy attends the day. Foggy out, sun felt without rain.
So help ye Conosess(?)

Monday 17th August 1778
Foggy morning however turned out at ye beat of ye drum. Gen. Cornell exercised his brigade a short time and were dismissed[140].
Then I was at Capt. Robinson's company and saw my friends. Some cannonading attends the day…

Tuesday 18th
Turned out at drum beating for roll call- A brief firing began the day.
Towards night I was Col. Carp(enter)s regiment & saw Capt. Willmarth's company.
Saw J. Stanley, E. Bacon, L. R(ichard)son and many others of my acquaintances. Heard my Father was well and friends at home-especially ye ladys…
Home & turned in…
Wednesday 19th August 1778
Turned out as usual-bought some Cheese & went to Capt. Willmarth's company & saw my friends…
Returned and cleaned my gun.
Cannonading continues-heard some of our men was killed at ye lines last night[141].

---

[140] On this date the Rhode Island General Assembley addressed the "happy prospect" of an expedition to "recover that part of the state now in the possession of the enemy", voting and resolving that "all the remaining part of the militia, independent and alarm companies, in this State, as well as officers, privates, …are now upon duty, or have hired others in their stead, be called forth to assist their bretheren upon Rhode Island". (State of Rhode Island and Providence Plantations, Council of War, August 17, 1778 Printed by John Carter, Providence 1778)

[141] In fact, despite a brisk firing of reportedly more than 300 shots upon the

About 8 o'clock was mustered out by the firing of small arms at ye lines…

Thursday 20th

Foggy morning however I wrote and sent a letter home by Mr. Barrow.

Washed my clothes.

Towards night Gen. Cornell's Brigade paraded for exercise. Cannonading attends the day. The French fleet returned to the harbor again…[142]

Friday 21st August 1778

About 3 o'clock this morning was mustered out by the firing of some small arms at the lines-turned in again directly-

Saw Col. Millers regiment surrounded by Col. Stephen's regiment.

Wrote a letter to N. Tiffany . Gen. Cornell's brigade paraded for exercise. Then went to Capt. Wilmarth's company…

Cannonading as usual

Sunday 23rd August 1778

Pleasant morning However cannonading begins ye day.

Orders for every tent to be struck at Ten o'clock by the Flar(e) of ye drum.

Heard the French Fleet had returned to N(ew)Port harbour who were driven out by the Great Storm at five o'clock.

men working to dig the trenches, only three were wounded, and a few American cannon disabled during the two nights the men worked under fire. (McBurney, p.144)

[142] The return of the French fleet would be brief. On the morning of August 20 Ensign Joseph Comte de Cambis went ashore on Point Judith to deliver the news that D'Estang and his squadron would leave for Boston for their damaged ships to be refitted. The Marquis de Lafayette, who strived to maintain the Franco-American alliance despite the rift the decision caused, would recall in his memoirs that "the council of pfficers held it to be their first duty, as naval commanders, to sustain the superiority of the French fleet on the ocean, to escape being shut up in port, and subjected to destruction by fire-ships, while at anchor in their disabled condition…"(Conley, Patrick T. *The Battle of Rhode Island: A Victory for the Patriots* Rhode Island History, Vol. 62,No.3,p. 55, McBurney, pp148-152, Arnold, HSRIPP Vol. 2., p. 424)

Pitched our tents again & saw J. Read & D. Hidn.
Heard one man died who was wounded yesterday[143]. At night
turned in to the Capt.'s tent.
 Nothing further at present…So help the Congress
Monday 24th August 1778
Cannonading……………………………
Turned out for Roll Call
Orders for a return of the men who had been in the Service
nine months to be made to the Col. &c.
I was at Capt. Wilmarth's company and borrowed ten dollars
of D. Hews(,) returned and saw my brother very unwell(.)
went and bought him some wine &c.
Heard the French Fleet had most certainly left ye harbour of
N(ew)port.
Orders for muster rolls to be made for the Regiment by ten
o'clock tomorrow.
In the evening took a walk and it appears to me we should
soon leave the Island.

Tuesday 25th August 1778
My brother remains unwell.
Went down to the guard and saw apt. Richardson then to
Capt. Robinson's & Willmarth's Company Then to my tent
and helped make the muster rolls-
Orders to be Ready to March at the shortest notice. Some
firing.

Wednesday 26th
Very warm & pleasant. I was at Capt. Willmarth's company
home and about ten o'clock had orders to parade our guns
and packs and be ready to march at the shortest notice.
Not much firing…in the evening some shells were hove…

[143] At about 1:30 am, an American picket post came under attack from
some 150 men of Colonel Edmund Fanning's Loyalist King's American
Regiment, killing one soldier with a bayonet and taking two others prisoner.
(McBurney, p. 160)

Thursday 27th August 1778
Got Breakfast and went to Capt. Willmarth's company. News was that the British Shipps were coming into Newport. Orders to parade as yesterday.
Lt. Bollock received a wound by a cannon ball hove by hand from our men, and went home.
Heard Col. Daggett was on the Island with a regiment.

Friday 28th
Heard there were two men killed at the line last night[144].
Was at Capt. Willmarth's company & saw J. Pullens & regiment. E. Daggett was at our camp and heard the folks were well at home.
At 2 o'clock a man was hanged in our camp[145].

Saturday 29th August 1778
Last night about 8 o'clock struck tents and returned back to the N. end of Island, about 9 o'clock an action began, the enemy pressing on our light party. It appeared there would be a general action however our Army looking for the rights of their country; fighting like heroes, the enemy dare not press on our main body[146].

---

[144] The night of the 27th two soldiers from Fanning's Regiment crept out to surprise two American sentries, and despite a loud struggle, killed them and returned to enemy lines. (McBurney, p. 161)

[145] On August 27, Drum Major Thomas Quigley of Webb's Regiment of Continentals was convicted of desertion and sentenced to hang the following day. Such severe punishment was unusual in the newly formed American Army whose ranks were deserted by roughly 1/3 of enlisted soldiers during the course of the war. Sullivan however, wished to set an example with a major battle looming. (McBurney, p. 161)

[146] Gen. Sullivan's line of defense while troops evacuated stretched for nearly two miles across the island.(McBurney, 170). The Massachusetts and Rhode Island troops under Gen. Cornell were posted behind stonewalls on the right wing of the line, while Col. Christopher Greene commanded another mixed brigade of regiments from Massachusetts and

About 4 o'clock ye Col. Bard marched down to the lines & lay by the wall. The action ceasing, we were exposed to no shot but Cannon which the God of Heaven directed from our heads.

Saw Capt. May & Camps.

Sunday, 30 August 1778

Last night returned to our former station (from the wall) and blanketed down. (Some cannonading on both sides) Dug an intrenchment, drawd provisions and Rum &c.

The loss of killed and wounded yesterday I can not certify but it appeared considerable on both sides[147].

Monday 31st

Last night mustered up about 5 o'clock, evacuated the lines. The whole Army crossed H(owland) Ferry. Encamped for the night (saw many of my acquaintences). Drawd Rum and provisions.

Some shot exchanged. Capt Hn. took Capt. Caleb's place...drew tents...

Tuesday 1st September 1778

Got Breakfast & struck tents.

New Hampshire taking up the center, and the left wing was commanded by John Glover, also posted behind stone walls on the eastern side of the island along the road to Butts Hill, the abandoned redoubt taken by the Americans, another 2,000 Massachusetts militiamen comprised of Titcomb's and Lovell's brigades formed a fall back line east and west behind the hill, while 500 yards to the north were another 800 Rhode Island militiamen. These were the last stand of defense before the route of retreat and Howland's Ferry. Robinson'sregiment was among the 120 men of Bristol County were in the rear guard with Titcomb's brigade. For full accounts of the battle, see McBurney, pp. 169-195, Arnold, HRIPP Vol. 2, pp.424-429, also Conley, TBRI, pp.54-65)

[147] British General Pigot's official report listed the combined losses of British, Hessian, and Loyalist troops to be 38 soldiers killed, another 210 wounded, with twelve missing. American casualties totaled 211, with 30 fatalities, 137 wounded, and fourty-four missing. (McBurney, p.195, Arnold, Vol. 2, p.428)

A number of Officers discharged in Col. Jacobs regiment among whom was Capt. Richardson, we were then put under Capt. Cole[148].

Packed up, took boat & sailed to Fall River[149] by 8 o'clock at night & bundled down, however the rain (?) us up & we pitched a tent.

Wednesday 2nd

Eat Breakfast of chocolate then went to Mr. Churches and bought some saus(age). Returned and packed up and moved on to hill east of Bardin's Tavern[150].

Pitched tent and faired very sumptuous for ye day.

Thursday 3rd September 1778

Turned out for roll call

Found I was (to) do the same duty with Capt. Cole as with Capt. Richardson.

Got Breakfast and went & bought some cucumbers.

Returned and washed my clothes.

Mr. E.Cn. & Seth. came in to camp from Attleboro.

---

[148] Captain Joseph Cole of Bridgewater began his service as Sergeant in Capt. Joseph Hayden's company of minute men, Col. Bailey's regiment, which marched on the alarm of April 19,1775. He would in turn serve as 1st Lt. in Capt. Elisha Mitchell's company from Feb. 21, 1776. By the time of Robinson serving as scribe, he was Captain in Col. John Jacobs regiment, serving 12mos. and 2 days in Rhode Island from Jan. 1, 1778 until Jan. 3, 1779. (MSSRW Vol. 3, pp. 773-774)

[149] Originally deeded on April 2, 1639 by Ossamequin (Massasoit) to twenty-six settlers and their heirs, the deed describes the boundaries as "all the tract of upland and meadows lying on the east side of the Taunton river, beginning or bounded toward the south with the river called the falls or Quequechand, and so extending itself northerly until it comes to a little brook called Stacey's Creek...to extend itself into the woods on a northeasterly point for four miles, and from the head of said four miles on a straight line southerly until it meet with the head of the four mile line at Quequechand...including all meadows, necks or islands lying and being between Assonate Neck and the Falls, aforesaid..." (The Phillip's History of Fall River, Fall River, Dover Press, 1944)

[150] The encampment is likely the site of what became the North Burial ground in Fall River.

Friday 4th

Pleasant morning. Drank Rum & Molasses with Mr. E. Capron & Seth[151].

Afterward heard his son set off for home with whom I sent a letter to CW(?)

Hear the British Fleet lay off nigh Boston Harbour.

Afternoon walked out of camp.

Saturday 5th September 1778

Bought some milk for Breakfast. Washed some clothes.

 Afternoon took a walk out of camp.

Sunday 6th

Had Chocolate for Breakfast

Went to Bardin's for writing

Heard the enemy landed five thousand of em' last night and burned the town of Bedford…[152]

---

[151] Elisha Capron (1737-1808) and his son Seth, (1762-1835) who served as a private in Capt. Joseph Cole's company, enlisted for five months in Rhode Island from July 5, 1778. He would later serve as drummer in Capt. Caleb Richardson's company of Col. John Hathaway's regiment, enlisting in January 1779, and as fifer in Capt. Joseph Franklin's company of Col. Nathan Tyler's regiment from August 25, 1779 until December 31, 1779. The following year he served 3months and six days in Rhode Island, once again with Capt. Caleb Richardson's company, with reinforcements to the Continental Army from late July until October 31, 1780. His final term of service came with Capt. Samuel Richardson's company of Col. Isaac Dean's regiment for 11 days in Rhode Island, from March 6th until his discharge on March 14, 1781. He later removed his family to Orange County, New York, where an impressive obelisk is erected in the Revolutionary veteran's honor. (MSSWR Vol. 3 p. 85, Find A Grave Memorial # 35446987

[152] The British landed four to five thousand troops at Clark's Cove on Saturday, September 5th piloted by a Dartmouth Tory, and led by a laborer into the largely abandoned town of Bedford. Soldiers marched down Middle Road, and then made their way on a path through the woods to County Road, and up to King Street. The troops then divided, with half marching along the river to Bedford village where they torched warehouses, barns, and houses. Other troops made their way into what is now South Dartmout, and burned houses there. According to Daniel Ricketson's History of New Bedford,"Almost everything went up in flames,

Had orders to be ready to move to Swansey tomorrow morning.

Towards night I went with R. St(anley) to Mr. Churches –got some cucumbers

At night went after Milk.

Monday 7th September 1778

Pleasant morning, so we packed up, put our baggage on board a boat & sent it over to Swansey[153], then marched & crossed Slades Ferry and took ground & pitched tents on a place called Hogsneck[154]. Afternoon did some writing. Baked beef for supper.

Tuesday 8th

Pleasant morning, so I went and bought milk and had rice for Breakfast, also for dinner.

Afternoon walked out of camp & bought some saus(age). Returned & eat rice and cucumbers at night. Concluded supper eating the fourth pot of rice for the day among six having no bread.

Wednesday 9 September 1778

---

the distillery was first, then 11 houses, 20 shops and one ropewalk, 7 ships, 1 barque, 1 snow, 8 brigs, 7 schooners, and 10 sloops. The brig *No Duty on Tea* totally on fire, floated up to Marsh Island and grounded there". (see also Desmarias, *The Guide to the American Revolutionary War in Canada and New England,* 142, and Roger Chartier, wwwwhalingcity.net)

[153] Corey and Hathaway Brightman whose farm lay adjacent to the ferry landing operated the ferry on the Swansea side of the Taunton River in conjunction with Slade's Ferry in Fall River. According to family records, "The first ferry boat was a canoe; later a raft was used; then a sailboat; and then the horse boat propelled by horses, and then it was manipulated by steam" (*Representative Men and Old Familes of Southeastern Massachusetts* Chicago, Beers & Co.1912 Vol. 3, p.1648)

[154] Robinson likely refers to the small peninsula that juts into what is now called Fox Hill Cove, just below the Army of the Grand Republic Highway (Rt. 6) as it led from the ferry into Swansea.

In the morning paraded and the company examined concerning Mr. Shearman's honey that was stolen last night. Eat rice & went with Corpl. Stanley to (?) for Mr. Slade[155]. Eat dinner in ye field then returned home in ye rain & eat potatoes and meat without bread having had none in the mess for two days.

Passed afternoon very rainey.

At night went after Milk & had bread etc.

Was very happy in eating bread and Milk then bundled down in peace.

Thursday 10th September 1778

This morning fair weather, so I went and carried Corpl. Stanley his breakfast and brought back some potatoes. Heard the enemy had landed and burndt Op's NTown[156].

Friday 11th September 1778

Swapt coats with Sergt. Vining[157]

Sergt. Smith set off home which brought orderly duty on the simple object-men went to Howland's Ferry after provisions.

---

[155]Obediah Slade of Swansea furnished the troops with supplies from the onset of the Newport invasion.. He would be captured by the British on the night of April 19, 1779 and witness the sight of his house burned by the redcoats, before being condemned to the prison ship *Jersey* where he would die in confinement. (Rose, Constance M. *Swansea in the War of the Revolution 1775-1783)* p. 29

[156] There is no indication that such an assault occurred, however camp rumours may have spread after word continued to come in of the British plundering of towns along the Acushnet River, including Fairhaven and Falmouth, as well as an expedition to Martha's Vineyard for livestock which successfully stole 10,000 sheep and 300 oxen for the troops in New York (Desmarias, 142)

[157] Likely George Vining of Bridgewater who enlisted as a private in Captain Reed's company of General John Thomas' regiment, April 27, 1775 serving three months, 1 week, and five days at Camp Roxbury. He later served in Capt. Nathan Snow's company of Col. Hawes regiment, which went on an expedition to Rhode Island. At the time of Robinson's journal, he was sergeant in Capt. Joseph Cole's regiment of Col. John Jacobs regiment, serving 11 months, 24 days in Rhode Island until his term expired on January 1, 1779(MSSRW, Vol. 16, p.336)

Several Swansey soldiers were sent for and brought in to camp[158].

At night called muster roll and turned out guard &c.

Saturday 12th September 1778

Arose and Called Roll. Doct. Billing came over and viewed the sick[159].

Afternoon shot at mark with Mr. L.(?) Willmarth

Supprawn for supper, having no bread…

Sunday 13th September 1778

Not having any bread we got supprawn for Breakfast.

One of Capt. Cole's company was confined (viz) Wm. Vose[160] Then I crossed the river with En(sign) Loring and completed ye muster rolls for Capt. Coles Company.

Brought back bread and had Baked beef for Dinner.

Paraded our Arms in order to be mustered. However, were not mustered for ye day, so we took up our arms and got Supper and turned in for ye night.

Monday 14th September 1778

Got Breakfast and turned out and was soon mustered by Kingsbury[161] muster, Master Gen(era)l Deputy.

---

[158] Swansea contributed 450 men and boys who served at one time or another during the war, these included the men who were called into Rhode Island, the most notable among them being Peleg Peck, and Philip Slade who led those troops in Bristol, Tiverton, and Warwick, Rhode Island. (Rose, *Swansea in the War of the Revolution*) p. 30

[159] Benjamin Billing served as Surgeon's Mate with Col. Benjamin Gill's regiment of Warner's brigade August 14, 1777 through December 12th of that year. He later served as Surgeon in Col. Isaac Dean's company on the alarm of July 31, 1780, serving 9 days at Tiverton Rhode Island until discharge on August 7, 1780.

[160] William Vose (1718-1778) served as a private in Capt. William Holden's company of Col. Robinson's regiment. The cause of his death at age sixty is unknown. (*Lineage Book- Daughters of the American Revolution* Vols. 55-56. Mrs. Euphemia Anderson Vose Hawes, # 54875)

[161] Likely Jacob Kingsbury of Norwich, Connecticut who had enlisted in the

Tuesday 15th
Sent a letter to my Father per favour of S. Richardson.
At night Sergt. Smith came in to camp & brought word my
Father and Brother were well…

Wednesday 16th September 1778
Turned out for Roll Call.
Two or three men were confined for firing in camp-had a fray
at ye narrow(s) after Pop(asquas)h[162]
Afternoon thrashed for M. Slade with Corpl. SV and (?) Ingals[163]
Settled our Mess Roll
Mr. Bardin came in to camp and Mr. Willmarth set off for
home.
(Mr. Bardin brought word my friends were in Health)
So much for ToDay

8th Connecticut regiment in 1775, which was incorporated into the
Continental line and served in the Seige of Boston. He was promoted to
Corporal, and integrated into the Continental Army after the regiment was
disbanded in December of that year. He served in that rank with Selden's
Connecticut State regiment from June to December 1776, and later served
as Ensign in Webb's Continental regiment, before being transferred to the
3rd Connecticut regiment, and then retained in Swift's Connecticut regiment
before ending his Revolutionary War service on November 3, 1783. He
would be assigned Lieutenant of the Unites States Infantry regiment in
November 1787, and earn his reputation in the Indian wars, and be one of
the few officers to srve in both the Revolutionary War and the War of 1812,
being discharged from the service on June 15, 1815. The muster master
was an officer or official placed in charge of muster rolls. (Heitman,
HROCA, p. 390, Coffman, Edward M. *The Old Army in Peacetime 1784-
1898* Oxford University Press 1986 p. 44)

[162] The narrows lie just south of Poppasquash point at the entrance to
Mount Hope Bay between Portsmouth and Bristol.

[163] Robinson and other militiamen were allowed to work day hours for
locals, as these men apparently took the opportunity when wheat needed
to be thrashed before it got wet and mouldy, or full of pests. Slade provided
for the officers and soldiers with both his tavern, and provisions like bread
and other goods to the soldiers coming and going on his ferry across the
Taunton River.

Thursday 17th September 1778

Last night very rainey however, R. St(anle)y & I had very good lodging there being no others in ye tent.

Was at Mr. Obidiah Slades and had my coat mended(,) bought some meal for supper. Likewise heard his youngest Lady (BG) sing songs.

Friday 18th

I was very busy in making pay rolls for Capt. Coles Company.

Saturday 19 September 1778

Finished ye rolls and got leave in part from Capt. Cole for R. Stanley and I for to go home so we get dinner and about 12 o'clock set out on our walk.

Marched to Anderson in Swansey drank some M. Punch then to Morses and drank grogg and Sangarea then home and was Happy to find my Father and Friends well.

So we got supper and R.S. & I turned in for the night.

Sunday 20th September 1778

Arose and drank an egg dram with R. St(anley)& was at Mr. Pullens & saw the Ladys.Then went to Meeting and heard Mr. Welds preach and saw many of my friends &c.

Return home after Meeting & got Supper then went to Adj. Daggetts and got grapes &c. Then went with R. St(anle)y to Mr. Pl.. where I left him with his HW(?) Delight However I returned home, turned in for ye night hearing Doct. Bliss was very sick...

Monday 21st September 1778

Arose and went with R. St(anley) to Mr. Richardson's (and) Drank rum then went to Lt. R(ichardso)n from thence to Mr. Perry's and received nine pounds L.M. of Lt. Rob(inso)n for my present services –then returned home & got Breakfast then went with R. Stanley to Mr. Whittiker's and drank very free with Mr. Willm(arth) & Pithikes(?) Then home & got Dinner then went to Mr. J. Dr(aper) and received pay for my work last summer & then to the W(illiam) St(anle)ys and Mr. Pullens then home & got Supper.

Then to Adj. Dagget's & got his horse then rhode up ye pastures from thence to B(enjamin)S(tanley) where I and my (?) then back and set off for the Falls S. House where we found a number of gents & Ladys carrying on in a very jovial manner. So the evening passed in jollity.

About 1 o'clock concluded Bang and every one to his own quarters.

I may mark well and Remember Y. Breeche (?)

Tuesday 22nd

Returned to Adj. Daggett and left his horse then walked on & met E. Daggett & R.E. Daggett. Returned to Mr. Richardson's where we had E(nglish). Rum &c.

Then home & got Breakfast,

In the forenoon was Roveing round with Eliz(abe)th Daggett[164] about 2 o'clock set off with R. Stanley for camp. Rode as far as Rehobeth anout 12 miles then walked & arrived in camp about 9 o'clock.

Wednesday 23rd September 1778

Arose and found the swine had eat(en) up my mess mates bread[165]. In the forenoon nothing remarkable happened Afternoon stormy, however pitched a tent and had liquor to drink.

Thursday 24th September 1778

---

[164] Likely the daughter of Mayhew Daggett (1730-1800) born in Attleboro who had raised a family in Dutchess County New York, but moved back to Attleboro after the death of his wife sometime after 1776. Elizabeth had married Jeremiah Reynolds of New York in 1773, and may have been visiting her father and extended family when Robinson met her. (Daggett Ancestors, Generation 8 rhead-burton connections.com retrieved 11/10/17)

[165] Common Ground, such as the grassy hill where the soldiers encamped were also used by foraging livestock, swine being the most prone to ravaging gardens and crops once loose, and in this case, an encampment.

Last night very stormy with some Thunder and Lightening
However clear this morning

Friday 25th
Arose and got Breakfast and did some writing &c.
About twelve o'clock my Father came in camp & brought me
some cheese paper &c. Went down to ye ferry with my Father.
Heard nothing remarkable....

Saturday 26th
Last night went the round with Sergt. Smith[166]. Returned &
bundled in.
Arose and drank a dram. Did some writing. Sent & bought
some Wool.
My Father returned...brought word my brother was well.
Father set out for home xbout twelve o'clock carried ye wool
however it was some rainey.

[166] Samuel Smith was born in Smithfiel, Rhode Island in 1759 but lived in the town of Middleboro, Massachusetts at the onset of the war and enlisted in 1776 as a private in the 1st Company of Infantry. He would serve in the Highlands, and at Red Bank in November of that year and spent the winter at Valley Forge. In the spring of 1778 he served as a medical assistant to Surgeon Elias Cornelius, and in that capacity served at the Battle of Monmouth. His regiment was sent to Rhode Island on August 25, 1778, and at the time of Robinson's writing, he was serveing as Sergeant in Capt. Perez Chrchill's company. At the close of the war he would make a living vicariously as a mariner and later as a baggage driver between Providence and Boston. Smith would write his own memoirs, which were published as a pamphlet in Middleboro in 1853, and later in hardcover by Charles Bushnell of New York, in 1860. (Smith, Samuel *Memoirs of Samuel Smith, A Soldier of the Revolution 1776-1786 Written By Himself* New York, Busnell, 1860 pp. 7-19, Weston, Thomas *History of the Town of Middleboro* Boston, Houghton Mifflin co. 1906 pp. 126, 134, 340)

Sunday 27th

Pleasant morning. Got Breakfast then sang a few tunes in Mr. Slade's house.

Lt. Bullock[167] came in to camp …..had cherry rum to drink.

The day passed in much carnality among ye soldiers in our camp

Towards night went after milk found two of Mess(?) mate in Misdemenior[168].

Monday 28th September 1778

Nothing remarkable happened in camp.

At night went on guard as a Sergt. for G. Stan(t)ly[169] and Rial Stanley as Corpl. for M. Bardin.

Tuesday 29th

Dismissed of Guard and Drank a dram and went to work for Mr. Chace[170] at noon. Heard a very comical discourse pass with Mr. Chace & his Lady Nab(by) Vose.

---

[167] Jabez Bullock of Rehobeth marched as 1st Lieutenant in Capt. Phanuel Bishop's company on the alarm of April 19, 1775. He was commissioned October 30, 1776 to serve in Col. homas Carpenter's 1st Bristol County regiment and marched to Bristol, Rhode Island on the alarm of December 8, 1776 , serving sixteen days. The following year he would serve with Capt. James Hill's company on a secret expedition to the state until October 30, 1777. At the time of Robinson's entry, he was serving as Lieutenant in Col. John Jacobs regiment, serving 3 months and 18 days until October 12, 1778. He would later serve as Captain of the 10th Company of Carpenter's regiment, commissioned April 13, 1779, and would serve in that capacity for 5 days in Tiverton, Rhode Island, and the following year another r9 days at Tiverton Under General Heith on an alarm. He was discharged on August 9, 1780. (MSSRW Vol 2, p. 795)

[168] Robinson interrupted some type of sexual act, what the courts in that time would have described as "lewd and lascivious conduct". Had Robinson reported them, they would have faced at the least a substantial fine, if not a whipping or expulsion from the army.

[169] Likely George Stantly, Corporal, Capt. Joseph Cole's Company of Jacob's regiment. He served 5 months, 27 days in Rhode Island from July 6, 1778 through January 1, 1779. (MSSRW Vol. 14, p. 833)

[170] Robinson likely worked at the store the Chace Family owned on Town Ave. B.W. Chace, who was a "dealer of domestics in every description",

At night took two dollars for my work and returned home. Eat Rice and Milk
Bundled in for the night.
Some disturbance in the mess. Mr. Bardin went home carried a letter to C. Stanley.
Wednesday 30th September 1778
Some Rain last night.
Got Breakfast and helped make new pay rolls. Finished the rolls by twelve o'clock and went immediately to Bardin's at Fall River and delivered em' to the Capt.
Tarried an hour or two then returned and got Dinner and went to writing again &c.
At sunset went after milk to Willbers Returned and bought bread for Supper Then turned in to our tents and then concluded in peace with the mess.

Thursday 1st October 1778
This morning was mustered out sooner than usual looking out for the Enemy by reason of some movements last night among the inhabitants of this place[171]. However discovered nothing remarkable.
Got Breakfast and went with Sergt. Smith to Brown's Tavern[172]

---

established the store in the early years of the town's development. His store was on the opposite corner of Colton's, another busy mercantile establishment. (*The History of Town Ave.* Historical Sketches of Fall River)

[171] There is no account of any action having taken place, but the entire region was under tension at this time, a company of Swansea men under Capt. Ward Smith having been sent to Falmouth and Dartmouth on alarms less than a month before. (*John Gibbs* Memorial Encyclopedia of Massachuseets Vol. 2, p 388, Revolutionary War Muster Rolls for the Town of Swansea, Bristol County, Massachusetts)

[172]The tavern was established by Major John Brown before 1769 when a group of five selectmen from Attleboro were sent to choose a new location for the Dighton Community Church. The group "rode on horseback, stayed overnight at Mr. Brown's tavern, looked over the sites, listened to everyone, and gravely chose a place no one favored. It was near a cart path that ran through an area called Buck Hill, somewhere near the center

Returning home bought some bread and had chocolate for Dinner.

Lt. Fuller & 10 men from Capt. Cole's Company went after deserters

Afternoon on did some writing. Very short for provisions.

Friday 2nd October 1778

This morning no bread so I went down to Chace's in order to work however was disappointed.

Returned back and Corpl. Stanley went after bread as we had neither bread, meat, or meal.

Before sunset Mr. Bardin came in to camp brought news my Father was well and that it was sickly in town among children.

After that Capt. Richardson was coming to Command his company & went after meal for to make supprawn so we lived the day with two meals of milk & supprawn.

Saturday 3 October 1778

Pleasant morning. Drew a qt of Rice for Breakfast &c.

Drew Bread and Meat for Dinner. Drank 2 quarts of wine at dineing in our mess-the (?) in the mess afterwards.

Did some writing in the evening, had some discourse with En(sign) L(oring).

Sunday 4th

Last night about 10 o'clock turned out, went the Rounds with Sergt. Smith

Discovered nothing remarkable (However, looked after Ch. R.S.)

Afternoon Capt. Richardson came in to camp brought word he was like to take his company again. Heard my brother was well per Sergt. Turner & Corp. Parker

---

of town". (Walkden. Marion B. *The Dighton Community Church* 1975, see also Lane, Helen Holmes *The History of Dighton, Massachusetts* Dighton, 1962)

Rainey.

Monday, 13th October 1778
Pleasant morning. Turned out and Capt. Richardson's generosity afforded the company a Grand treat of Rum(,) Wine &c.
Went after milk and got Breakfast. Capt. Richardson set off from camp.
Afternoon went over to Fall River heard eleven tories was then sent to Providence[173].
Sent a letter to my brother dated ye 6 of this instant, Returned and saw two tories brought in to camp.
In the evening was in Mr. Slades house and Heard Sergt. Watkins[174] discourse and the Ladys sing....
Tuesday 6th October 1778
Sergt. Smith going off to Taunton with the tories brought orderly duty[175] on me wherefore I was obliged to keep to my quarters.

---

[173] Likely part of the more than one hundred and fifty British and Hessian prisoners that would be sent to Acquidneck Island the following month, in exchange for the safe removal of over 150 inhabitants, as well as "upwards of 100 prisoners...went on board a Cartell for Providence" from Newport on November 29, 1778. (*Newport in the Hands of the British*, The Historical Magazine, May 1860, Vol IV, no. 5. p. 135)

[174] Zachariah Watkins first served as Sergeant on the Lexington alarm in April 1775. He would serve as Sergeant-Major in Thompson's company of the Massachusetts militia the remainder of that year. He would serve as 2nd Lieutenant in the 23rd regiment of the Continental line the fllowing year, and as a Lieutenant in the militia from 1777-1779. Robinson's reference to him as "sergeant" may be from familiarity rather than an indication of his present rank at that time. (Heitman, p. 575)

[175] That is, the keeping of the "orderly book" of the company, as per the regulations set forth by New England Army Commander Atremus Ward, the documentation of the day-to day life within an army encampment. General Orders, from General Washington's headquarters were usually dicatated early in the day at the Adjunct General's office. Later, Garrison orders, or Missives from departmental Commanders would also need to be copied as well as any reports issued that day relating to the company.

Spent the day chiefly in writing.

Wednesday 7th
Roll Call and got Breakfast. Was very busy in writing. Col.
Pope[176] came to camp & made out a provision return &c.
Was informed we ware to march to H(owlands) Ferry next
Friday.
Sergt. Smith came in and relieved me of my duty.
At night went after milk &c.

Thursday 8th October 1778
Dressed ye Capt's Hair[177] & was very busy in writing.
Received the Capt's favor concerning DJas up Cumb (?)
The Drunken Malliton Fray to be remembered.

Friday 9th
Turned out and our milk being sower we ware obliged to
March off without breakfast. Marched to B(ard(i)n(s). & found
two more companies then marched below H. Ferry to Quakit[178]
and found the regiment.

(Robertson, McDonald, *A Brief Profile of Orderly Books* www.revwar.com)

[176] Col. Edward Cole commanded the 2nd regiment of the Bristol County militia.

[177] Though an officer might wish to remain a gentleman, it was more practicle in camp to have someone dress the natural hair to resemble a *peruke*, or wig in the fashion of the time, as did General Washington himself. (Galke, Laura *Perukes, Pomade and Powder: Haircare in the 1700's* Lives and Legacies blog, Ferry Farm https://livesandlegaciesblog.org/2015/01/28/perukes-pomade-powder/)

[178] Likely the area above, and alongside Nannaquaket Pond, as the long, marshy inland cove is called. Its narrow inlet from Mount Hope Bay was called the "Quacket River".

Saw my brother however did not speak to him for ye day then joined Genl. Cornell Brig. Drawed sporting cartridges and fired them away in the most warlike manner in imitation of a field action (in the presence of Genl. Sullivan & his attendents) The sun about two hours high, marched for our own camp. Marched to Simmons and got Supper, then to Bardin's and made a short stop then put on and got home very much fatigued about 9 o'clock at night and turned in....

Old Cushmans Box Blew up and Sweet he did Fla-ha ha-[179] Nothing further singular only not speaking to my brother when I was within five miles of him and had not seen him for forty days before...

Saturday 10 October 1778

Windy and Cloudy, cold.

After buying about three dollars worth, we draw'd bread & meat, soap, candles, etc.

Reckoned in the mess.

Afternoon Rainey. At night went after milk...

Kept to my tent chiefly for ye Day.

Sunday 11th October 1778

Last night very stormy.

However had several laughs about Mr. Cush' Box blowing up[180] then about R St(anley)'s singing...Had milk for Breakfast and it being a very stormy day we kept our tent and spent ye day very carnally.

---

[179] Likely Zenas Cushman(1743-1799(?) of Middleboro, whose name appears on the list of the 1st Company of Minute Men from Middleboro under Capt. William Shaw, whose company several times in Rhode Island. At the close of the war, Cushman seems to have been given a clerical role, as he is listed as having signed for payments to soldiers for their time of service. (Weston, Thomas *History of the Town of Middleboro, Massachusetts* Cambridge, The Riverside Press 1906 pp. 120, 126)

[180] A common enough problem during the war, when an exposed cartridge box was easily ignited from a spark fallen from the flash pan of a soldier's musket. A remembrance of soldier Richard Pugh, of Floyd County Virginia is one example. Pugh at the age of twenty-one, " enlisted as a private in the Continental line. He fought in the Battle of Eutaw Springs and was

Milk for supper & turned in by dark.

Monday 12th October 1778
This morning clear and cold.
Lt. Fuller came in to camp and brought word Capt.
Richardson was not to take his company again.
Did some writing &c.
In the evening took a walk with Capt. Fuller.
Had considerable talk with him. Heard my brother was well.
Tuesday 13th
Did some writing-Made muster rolls.
Heard nothing remarkable
At night went after milk
In the evening heard Ensign Loring[181] tell stories about ye old
woman and ye tommorow Seter...[182]

Wednesday 14th
Pleasant morning. In the forenoon was busy in writing.
Col. Pope came to our camp.
Afternoon E. Will(marth) came into camp & Mr. Bardin set off
home by whom I sent a letter to my Father.

---

wounded in service by an exploding cartridge box..." (Floyd County Virgina
Heritage Book 2000 *The Pugh Family of Floyd County* pp. 138-139)

[181] Joshua Loring of Plympton enlisted June 10, 1776 as a sergeant in
Capt. Thomas Turners company of Col. Thomas Marshall's regiment,
serving 5 months and 27 days through December 1, 1776. He later
appears on the list of men mustered by James Hatch of Plymouth
company, and served as sergeant in Capt. Joseph Cole's company of
Robinson's regiment for 5 months and 29 days in Rhode Island through
January 1, 1778. On that day he was appointed Ensign for service in the
same regiment for another twelve months, and was on the "list of officers
appointed to command two regiments raised for the defence of the New
England states and commanded by Col. Wade and Col. Jacobs". (MSSRW
Vol. 9, pp. 969-970)

[182]Refers to the Jewish feast of Seder, a time of eating specially prepared
foods, singing, story-telling, and drinking wine throughout.

Towards night I went after bread & milk. Got some milk and returned without bread.

Thursday 15th
Went and bought some bread for breakfast then went writing in which I spent ye most part of (the) day.
Towards night went down to ye ferry with Sergt. Smith. Saw Col. Jacobs...[183]

Friday 16th
Windy & cold ye morning.
Drew Allowance...did some writing

Saturday 17th
Did some writing. Nothing singular passed for ye day.

Sunday 18th
Cool Morning.
Went to Mr. Wilbur's after milk & got Breakfast then went to making pay rolls.
Afternoon, Capt. Coles Company was mustered by Maj. Kingsbury.

Monday 19th
Pleasant morning.

---

[183] Col. John Jacobs of Scituate, Massachusetts, was commissioned Major in Gen. Thomas' regiment of the Plymouth County militia May 19, 1775. He would later serve as 2nd Major Col. John Thomas' regiment at Roxbury. He was appointe Lieutenant Colonel in Col. John Robinson's regiment May 8, 1777, and recommissioned on December 8th of that year. On Marcxh 2, 1778 he was appointed Colonel of the regiment raised for service in Rhode Island, from April 1, 1778 through December 31st, a total of 9 months. The following year he would serve as Colonel of a regiment of light infantry from May 15, 1779 through November 19, 1779. He would be commissioned on June 22, 1780 as Colonel among a list of officers appointed to command men detached from their militia to reinforce the Continental Army for three months. He was discharged on November 3, 1780 following 3 months and 29 days of service. (MSSRW Vol.8, p. 699)

Got Breakfast and finished ye pay rolls for Capt. Cole's Company.

The Capt. went to Fall River with said rolls. They being wrong (,) the Capt. returned with em' and we set to making new rolls until about 9 o'clock then turned in.

Oliver Blackn'[184] returned from Attleboro

Heard nothing remarkable only the Lady generally in Health.

Tuesday 20th October 1778

Awoke and Drank a Dram and went to making pay rolls (however was some(what) unwell). Got the rolls done by 10 o'clock.

There was some difficulty with ye Capt. and some of his men concerning S. Cole & Stanley's doing duty & Sergt. Bicknell's going home.

Towards night did some writing for myself. Had a discouse with (?)

Wednesday 21st October 1778

Pleasant morning so I got Breakfast and went to Lt. Shearman to Horse Neck[185] had a very good dinner and Grogg & at night returned to camp and turned in without supper.

NB. R. Stanley went on Guard...

Thursday 22nd

---

[184] Oliver Blackinton marched on the alarm of April 19, 1775, and later served as private in Capt. Moses Willmarth's company of Daggett's regiment. At the time of Robinson's writing, he was serving in Capt. Joseph Cole's company of Col. John Jacobs regiment for 5 months, 27 days at Rhode Island ending January 1, 1779. He would end his service the following year in Capt. Enoch Robinson's company of Dean's regiment, discharged on August 8, 1780.

[185] Most likely the area between present day Allens Pond and the peninsula still called Horse Neck that juts out into the Westport River.

Pleasant morning however we had not any bread so we sent after meal for suppawn and I went after milk and had a very sumptuous Breakfast then set off with Corpl. Stab(?) after some Ellibore[186].

Took the fatigue of walking about four or five miles and returned without any-at last being very hungry we dined on potatoes & beef.

Suppawn for Supper then had some singing in our tent with Ensign Loring & Sergt. Smith. (heard Doctor Cook of Norton was dead[187]). Heard Ensign Loring tell the story concerning an old woman being eighty-four years of age and had in mind to change her condition.

Friday 23rd October 1778
Lousy & cold morning.
Having not any bread we eat potatoes & milk for Breakfast-drew Allowance for nine days &c.

Capt. Cole brought orders we ware to have no more furloughs at present.

Afternoon did some writing.. Wrote to E. Loring's. Drew mutton.

Heard the enemy seem to be on some what of a movement, however what was their design was uncertain.

Went after milk at night.

Saturday 24th October 1778
Lousy and cool morning.
In the forenoon did some writing

---

[186] Possibly *elebore* or more commonly *hellebore*, a flowering plant long believed to have medicinal properties for both purging the body of toxins as well as for some skin irritations.

[187] Dr. Nathaniel Cook was the son of Paul and Joanna Cook, born May 29, 1752. He died on October 22, 1778. (Hurd, Dwayne Hamilton, ed. *History of Bristol County Massachusetts with Biographical Sketches of Many of its Pioneers and Prominent Men* Philadelphia, J.W. Lewis & Co. 1883 Vol. 2, p. 621)

Afternnon went after W(all)Nuts with Corpl. Stanley.
Towards night Major Brown & some other officers came in to camp & brought news the enemy were all afloat from (New) York, and that we must not be permitted out of camp[188].
Sent after milk at night.
Sunday 25th
Lousy morning. In ye forenoon nothing new passed, dined with Mr. Slade (on Roast Goose) then went to Mr. Wilbur's & drank cyder.
Returned & had baked mutton &c.
In the evening had a sing with Ensign Loring burning straw &c.
Monday 26th
Pleasant morning. In the forenoon carried my cloathes to be washed. Took a walk with Sergt. Smith &c.
Dined on Baked mutton afterward Uncle Jn Stanley[189] came in to camp & brought word my Father and folks were well. (brought in some hell timber &c)

---

[188] Rumors of the British navy's intentions were circulating as early as the first week of October. A letter sent to General Washington from Horatio Gates on October 6th, speculates that the British might be aiming for Boston and the French fleet, as well as a letter that same day from Charles Scott telling of an engagement between the British and French near Bedford, New York. By the middle of the month, a letter from Elias Dayton to Major General William Alexander, and passed along to Washington, surmises that South Carolina couls also be an intended target of the British fleet. On October 18th, there were rumors of the British evacuation of New York, and preparations were intensified for an anticipated attack on Boston. Word of movements of the fleet continued to por into Washington's headquarters. On the 22nd General John Sullivan received word that a flag of truce had been brought to Rhode Island, an indication that an evacuation was imminent. As the month war on howver, little of significance occurred and the correspondence tiurns to the preperations of winter and the procurment of provisions and clothing. (Fitzpatrick, Clement *Calendar of the Corrrespondence of George Washington Commander in Chief of the Continental Army with The Officers* Washington, Library of Congress 1915 Vol. 1, pp 777-802. Vol. 2, pp. 803-822)

[189] Jonathan Stanley was the younger brother of Deborah Stanley Robinson, Noah's mother. See earlier footnote.

In the evening was at Mr. Slade's & saw the dance and heard the fiddle.

Tuesday 27th October 1778
This morning some Lousy-
Turned out and drank a dram with ye Deacon[190] then fried mutton for breakfast.
About 10 o'clock the Deacon set off for home by whom I sent a letter to E. Daggett &c.
Afternoon was preparing for a toast in ye old schoolhouse, got fixed and about (?) o'clock began ye seage. Continued ye Tast till about 12 o'clock. Tended by Corpl. Stanley & O. Bn. then cleaned up,
during the seage used two quarts of Rum-turned in & slept.
Part of company moved to (?)

Wednesday 28th
Pleasant morning……...
Awoke and dressed in clean clothes However the smell of the weapon was not quite exhausted.
In the afternoon went with Corpl. Cooper[191] after nuts.
In the evening eat the same. Did without bread for the day.
Thursday 29th October 1778
Lousy morning.
Went after milk for Breakfast and had suppawn.
In the forenoon reckoned in the mess, then with Rial &c.

_____

[190] He again, refers to his Uncle Deacon Jonathan Stanley, a life long congregant of the 1st Congregational Church.

[191] David Cooper of Attleboro enlisted as a private in Capt. Stephen Richardsons company on April 21, 1777, serving twenty-five days in Rhode island through May 15th. He would later enlist and march on a "secret expedition" into the state from September 25, 1777 through October 29th. At the time of Robinson's writing, he was serving as Corporal in Capt. Joseph Cole's company of Col. Jacobs regiment, enlisting on July 6, 1778 for five months and twenty-seven days. (MSSRW Vol. 3, p. 975)

Towards night went with Corporal Stanley to Mr. Slades then returned and bought a quart of milk of Mr. Slade for which I may thank Mr. Sally & Ruth.

In the evening began a sing when O. Bk & Sr's tent got on fire & burnt Oliver's hair very much & caused a considerable combusture in camp[192].

Friday 30th October 1778
Last night was a false alarm
Lousy morning, however got breakfast & went across the river to Bardin's for orders with Capt. Cole.
Returned for Dinner
Turned out for Exercise and met the remainder of company in order for a sham fight
However they soon got into a dispute and ye affair dropt-then exercised a while and Sergt Smith's party marched in ground divisions Round Sw(ansea) then come home with flying colors[193].

---

[192] The unfortunate Oliver Blackinton, see earlier footnote.

[193] A Sham Fight was a time honred tradition, and part of militia training as the *Directions for a General Training Exercise for the Boston Militia (1686)* demonstrates. As reprinted in John Demos' *Remarkable Providences*, the manual illustrates in great detail every stage leading up to the fight: After forming, the troops march to the common and perform a series of maneuvers, the culmination of which requires *the whole body now move forward and approaching within 50 paces, trail their pikes, still moving slowly forward, and begin to fire, first by two files ranking from each flank before the body, reducing themselves next the pikes, then rankwise, the whole body moving up and the pikes charging, sometimes one retreating and then the other, as the drums give notice, but none approaching nearer than ten paces of both arms. In the heat of which all the horse, joining together, interpose, and drums beat a retreat of all hands, face about, and move to a convienient distance; drums beat a triumph; colors flourishing; then (if any minister be there) draw together as before, and so into a circle as before, and pray.*

Then every Capt.receiveth his own company, marcheth home, and lodgeth his colors.

(Demos, John *Remarkable Providences: Readings on Early American History* (Revised Edition) Boston, Northeastern University Press 1972,

Saturday 31st October 1778

Lousy morning-rainey-

In the fore part of the day nothing singular passed only I wrote a letter for Sergt. Smith.

Afternoon walked with Smith down to Cottons and saw the remainder of ye company.

returned & eat beef, bread & potatoes then spent some time in writing.

At night had not any bred for supper –In the evening was alone in my tent and wrote the aforesaid remarks of the day the bundled down.

Sunday 1st November 1778

Behold! the first Day of ye Month and the first Day of the week is now began; which comes in with a Cold & Lousy Morning and we destitute of Bread.

So I went down to J(oh)n Wilbers & bought two (loaves) of Bread.

Returned to eat Breakfast & Shucked (Shell) Fish & potatoes for dinner.

Dined without bread & nothing material passed in our camp for ye day.

In ye evening, Ensign Loring was at our tent and some jollity passed…drew bread & eat & turned in for the night.

Monday 2nd November 1778

Last night & this Morning very stormy, However I turned out and went down to the shore after meat &c.

Returned back very wet, however eat some milk & bread and bundled in to blanket to dry my self- it being rainey.

Nothing new passed in our camp only Armt. & Em_ss(?) being confined supposing they stole Meat last night which was Null…

In the evening had considerable dialogue with Mr. W(illmar)th.

Sunday 3rd November 1778

1991 pp. 290-293)

Pleasant morning. Turned out & washed my shirt & stockings &c.

Then went and crossed the ferry to Bardin's (with Sergt S.B.) and bought some paper

Then took Boat Back and jumping out, the boat miscarried and got wet legs.

At night turned out the guards.

In the evening Capt. Cole and Ensign Loring was at our tent. Some singing passed, then I went ye Rounds with Ensign Loring & had some dispute with St. Swg(?)

Wednesday 4th November 1778

Cool morning, however I mended my shirt and breeches & shifted my cloathes[194] & went to writing in which I spent the forenoon.

Dined on Baked Beef then paraded the Company for Exercise & towards night ten men from _____ joined Capt. Coles company…

In the evening reckoned with Sergt. Smith then went to Mr. Slades House and some jollity passed (in my) (?) to RS Ru(?)

Thursday 5th 1778

The morning winday; also some(what) wet & lousy

In the forenoon wrote a Letter and sent to my Father to favour Capt. Stanley who set off for Attleboro about noon.

Afternoon drew bread…

Friday 6th

Was very busy in making muster rolls for Capt. Cole's company

At night got milk of Mr. Slead, & eat supper & turned in…….

Saturday 7th November 1778

---

[194] Prepared what wardrobe he had for winter. This would have included extra shirts or shifts to wear beneath his extra layer of clothing.

The latter part of the night last, very extremely rainey with some Thunder (at a distance). The morning continues the same, however I got Breakfast and went to making pay rolls of Capt. Cole's company in which I spent the main part of the day. About noon the storm abated.

Sunday 8th November 1778

Pleasant morning so we arose and Drank a Dram and got Breakfast & I went to making out pay rolls-

Afternoon took a walk with Sergt. Smith after Nuts.

Returned and saw L. Stan(ley) who brought word my Father was well, and the ladies in good plight…

Got milk of Mr. Slade for supper & in the evening had some singing with Ensign Loring & Sergt. Smith by the side of the wall…then turned in & wrote the aforesaid remarks.

Monday 9th November 1778

This morning rainey, however in the forenoon I busied myself in drafting a vessel at the end of this book…

Dined on beef & potatoes without bread.

Toward night drew some bread with difficulty, bought some milk for supper &c.

Tuesday 10th

Pleasant morning. Suppawn for Breakfast then wrote a letter to send to (?)

Afternoon drew provisions…towards night our company passed muster. Saw Col. Jacobs, heard my brother was well….boatmen[195] called out…joined our company.

Wednesday 11th November 1778

[195] Boatmen in the Continental Army were enlisted in "amphibious regiments", the most famous being General John Glover's 14th Continental regiment of Marblehead fishermen. These men were essential in piloting troops across estuares and salt-water channels, as well as espionage, and espeditions against enemy shipping. The boatmen mentioned here were of Churchill's regiment, of which Samuel Smith was a member as seen below. (Kuhl, Jackson *The Whale-Boat Men of Long Island* Journal of the American Revolution, November 2013)

Last night about 10 o'clock we were ordered out of our tent by the sentry telling us there was (an) alarm, however, we thinking he was about to fool us(,) did not turn out at his call- Then was called by Sergt Smith which was to no purpose, then was ordered out by the Capt. which we reddily obey'd. Turning out in our flaps then the officers gave us a drink of grogg and told us they had nothing further for us but onley to turn in again (thus they served all in our camp) then the officers took a bottle of rum with them and went the rounds, meanwhile they carried on very jovial, takeing guards & sentry's &c.

They firing whole Platoons at a Sloop to bring her too[196]. Alarmed us in camp so we turned out & paraded, marched towards them till the firing ceased then returned and bunked in, it being about two o'clock.

Day appearing we turned out and got Breakfast and a very rainey day ensued.

In the forenoon did some writing then reckoned in the mess and drank Rum &c.

Mr. Bardin came in to camp and Mr. Wilmarth went home..

Thursday 12th November 1778

Pleasant morning.

In the forenoon wrote a letter to send to JD. with one inclosed directed to Mrs (?)

Afternoon warned the guard & went down to the shore and hauled up a boat. At night turned out the guard; then had considerable discourse in our stone parley...

Friday 13th

Very pleasant morning.

---

[196] Sergt. Samuel Smith would write in his memoir "In the course of the winter of 1778, many of the regiment to which I belonged were taken to go on ship board, to run down the river to attack and take the Britsih shipping which lay there. The ship that I went on board of had two cannons. Our orders were to run alongside of the British shipping, board, and take them". (Smith, Samuel *Memoirs of Samuel Smith*...p.16)

I saw Mr. Davis Levy set off for Attleboro by whom I sent the aforesaid letters

In the forenoon I went down to Cottons[197]

Returned & had Baked Beef for dinner, drew bread, rice, molasses, then sent up to Mr. Slead for milk (?) & c. then bundled in to our tent on new straw.

Saturday 14th

Last night very stormy, however we lodged very well in our tent and arose this morning and found fair weather- eat Breakfast of rice & milk &c.

In the forenoon did some writing

Afternoon Col. Pope came over to our camp.

Mr. Bardin & RS went out & sold some fish & bought cabbage & candles &c.

Sunday 15th November 1778

This morning very cold with some flakes of snow-Ensign Loring has returned who was called out with a boat party on the tenth of this (month?) and on his passage for Greenwich had been cast on to Prudence and eight of our company were missing besides others from other companies, supposing to be cast on the same place or to R. Island & made prisoners or drowned, most certainly one of the three is their fate.

I had an invitation to go with Lt. Fuller to Warren to see if we could hear of them-it being cold I went not…

---

[197] Coltons Store, established by John S. Colton on the corner of Town Avenue and Market Street, carried an extensive variety of goods and was a gathering place for marketmen. The intersection where the store was located would eventually become known as "Colton's Corner". (*The Story of Town Ave.* Historical Sketches of Fall River, p. 8)

Mr. Bardin being unwell I went with him to Capt. Shearman[198]'s where he got liberty to stay-so I bought of Quart of Milk & returned and eat supper (the RS & Rmber) Then turned in to sleep &c.

Monday 16th
Got Breakfast and went to draughing a ship in which I spent the forenoon.
afternoon the barrak master came and barruk'd ye company so we struck our tent and took barrak at E.L. Wilbers, got supper and went to Mr. Shea'
Returned and Rial & I turned in to a feather bed for sleep.

Tuesday 17th
Pleasant Morning.
I got Breakfast and imployed myself in Draughing a ship at Mr. Slades.
At Noon Returned to Mr. Wilber and dined with him. Then returned to Mr. Slade's and spent the remainder of the day. In the evening Sergt. Smith came to our quarters and some dispute passed with Mr. Wilber concerning singing...
About 9 o'clock we turned in to a bed as last night.

Wednesday 18th November 1778
Last night rainey and lousey this morning.

---

[198] Capt. Peleg Shearman of Swansea began his military career as 1st lieutenant, Capt. Caleb Hill's 2nd company of the 1st Bristol County Regiment under command of Col. Thomas Carpenter, serving 104 days. He would later serve as Captain in the same company, stationed as guards at Slade's Ferry in Swansea throughout much of 1777. During that year he served 34 days in North Kingstown, Rhode Island, as well as 6 days in October on a secret expedition. On June 17, 1778 he was commissioned as Captain of the 2nd Company, 1st Bristol County regiment. At the time of Robinson's writing, he served as 2nd Lieutenant in Capt. Joseph Cole's company of Col. John Jacobs regiment, in Rhode Island from June 27, 1778 through January 1, 1779, a total of six months and three days. (MSSRW Vol. 14, pp 86-87)

So I busied my self in draughing my ship which I completed by suns setting.

I heard the lost boatmen before mentioned were found...

In the evening heard a lady read the Arabian Nights entertainment, and tell some interesting stories.

Heard Col. Jacobs regiment was all on Fall River shores(,) which had him stationed at Little Compton.

Thursday 19th November 1778

Arose and went up to Roll Call.

Returned and eat Breakfast and about 10 o'clock my brother & Wm Bkton & Corpl. Parker came over from Tiverton shore, whom I had not spoke with for two months and nineteen days.

They stay(e)d and dined with us, they tarried with us four or five hours which time passed with a very agreeable conversation....

Some (?) my comrades being gone I walked out & saw my acquaintances..

Returned in the evening, much discourse & many arguments passed with Mr. Wilber & G. Shearman[199] on diverse subjects. Some snow.

Friday 20th November 1778

Arose and got Breakfast went over to Slades Ferry with Mrs. Sinthy(?) and saw the ship[200].

---

[199] George Shearman (1749-1808) was born in Dartmouth, Massachusetts. He married Seaford Gifford on October 28, 1770 in that town. He would later live in New Bedford where he died sometime before December 2, 1808. (*Vital Records of Dartmouth, Massachusetts to the Year 1850* Vol. 1, p. 223, *Ibid,* p.426, *New Bedford Mercury* December 2, 1808)

[200] Robinson identifies the ship he drew as the *Elert,* a two-masted brigantine under a flag that may be an early naval ensign.

Returned & got Dinner & spent some time in writing, then some hours discourse with Mr. Wilber- towards night I should have gone over to Fall River after the Ensign but having no boat, I went to Ensign Loring who supplied me...
Returned and passed the evening mostly in reading &c. Thus time passed very pleasant(ly).

Saturday 21st November 1778
Very pleasant morning so we got Breakfast and I went over to Sergt. Smith's quarters then we back'd up some wood from the shore[201].
Dined on baked beef, then I went to Mr. Slade's
Returned & did some writing.
At night Lt. Fuller was at out quarters & gave me some incouragement of going home &ccc.
The evening passed chiefly in discourse with Mr. Wilber...

Sunday 22nd November 1778
This morning very cold, however got Breakfast and went to Mr.Slades.
Ensign Loring returned and dined with us. Afterward spent some hours in discourse.
Passed the remaining part of the day in reading.
The evening passed with some singing.

Monday 23rd
Lousy Morning.
Lt. Fuller came & called us out of bed for Revelle to go after wood.
Corpl. SV (?) came into camp and brought a letter from my Father dated the first of this month.

---

[201] Stacked driftwood at the edge of the beach.

Towards night I took a walk with Sergt. Smith up to Capt. Anthony's[202] & drank coffee then returned and took a walk with Lt. Fuller & Smith to Hog Neck, returned and got leave in part for R(ial) S(tanley) and I to go home.

Found my brother at our quarters with a furlough to go home tomorrow, so he supped with us and the evening passed very pleasant and we were all very well pleased with our tomorrow's proposal....about 10 o'clock turned in for sleep.

---

[202] Burrington Anthony was a captain of the Portsmouth Militia, appointed in 1775. He was taken prisoner by General Richard Prescott, commander of the occupying British forces in May 1777, and thrown in jail in Newport, where Prescott visited him often and mused aloud on the day when the patriot would be hung. Those plans were foiled however, by the capture of Prescott humself, during a daring raid orchestrated by Col. William Barton of Tiverton. Anthony repeatedly refused to take the oath of allegience to Great Britain and was held in prison for more than a year. (Zilian, Fred *Looking Back at Our History: An Enterprise Agaist the Enemy* Newport Daily News, July 8, 2017, and Stone, Edward Martin, *Our French Allies, Rochambeau and his Army, Lafayette and his Devotion, D'Estaing DeTerney, Barras, DeGrasse and their Fleets in the Great War of the American Revolution from 1778-1782*, Providence, 1884 p.102)

Tuesday 24ᵗʰ November 1778
Awoke very early Marched for home by Day light marched as
far as Mr. Goff's in Rehobeth[203] about twelve miles w(h)ere we
had a very good Breakfast on freecost(,) then marched on to
Doriah's and drank some brandy, the Richardson's tavern and
drank egg pop then put on to Col. Richardson[204]'s and dined
with him-then put on through the neighborhood and found
my friends all well and I was happy to find my Father in the
same state.

In the evening some of my friends came in to see me & then I
went to Mr. Pullens. From thence home with RJS and lodged
with him, after we had turned in about half an hour Sall W. &
S. Richardson came to the window to speak with us so we let
them in and had considerable discourse on several affairs....

Wednesday 25ᵗʰ November 1778
Arose and found a very pleasant morning, so I went from
Uncle J(onathan)'s to Mrs Barrows who gave incouragement
of Make(ing) me some breeches.

---

[203] Likely the residence of Samuel Goff, who settled in Rehoboth about
1720. His son Samuel Goff Jr. would serve in the county's militia
companies throughout the war. What is now known as the Goff Homestead
(circa 1750) remains in Rehoboth, though it is uncertain that this is the
house visited by Robinson and his fellow militiamen.

[204]Colonel Stephen Richardson of Attleborough was commissioned a Lt.
Colonel on June 26, 1776 for Colonel Simeon Cary's regiment, and was
among the list of officers "raised for Quebec and New York". He is also on
the list of Attleboro men who served for 5 months in what became known
as the "6ᵗʰ campain" at York later that year. Though content to be at home,
and perhaps operating a tavern during the soldier's visit, he would be
reappointed as Lt. Colonel in Col. Abiel Mitchell's regiment on July 30,
1780 detached from Bristol County for 3 months and 21 days service in
Rhode Island, as reinforcements for the Continental Army. He was
discharged from duty on October 30, 1780. (MSSRW Vol. 13, p. 267)

Then I returned and got Breakfast and set out with Mr. R(ial S(tanley)-on a walk first to Doct. Man(n)s then to Mr. Days, from thence to Capt. May'[205]s and dined and received fifteen pounds in money & then went ro Mr. Drapers & saw the Ladies then to Mr. Bliss's on business; then to Aunt BDA's then home & supped.

In the evening walked up to Adj. D(agge)tts & spent some hours discourse and returned to Uncle J's for lodging.

Thursday 26th November 1778

Arose and found a very pleasant morning (which was of great satisfaction in general) it being a day set apart for a day of Prayer & Thanksgiving[206].

Returned home and sent of a shirt to be made; and got Breakfast and went to Mrs. Barrows to have some work done. Returned and changed my cloathes & walked to meeting with ye Ladies & R(ial) S(tanley) and heard Mr. Weld (however his discourse was half past), saw many of my acquaintances....

---

[205] Elisha May (1739-1811) of Attleboro was a farmer and held several local offices during his lifetime, including selectman, coroner, justice of the peace, and state representative. At the outbreak of the war he was a sitting member of the Committee of Correspondence, as well as serving as a state senator (1778-1804). May served in the Massachusetts Militia, commissioned a Lieutenant in Jabez Ellis' company, he would later serve as captain in John Daggetts regiment, and as major, lieutenant colonel, and colonel in Isaac Dean's 4th regiment of Bristol County. (*Biographical Sketches,* May Family Papers, Massachusetts Historical Society, MSSRW Vol. 10, p. 375)

[206] Despite the date, the holiday we know as "Thanksgiving" was not an officially declared holiday on the last Thursday of the month until 1863. Prior to Lincoln's pronouncement after years of lobbying efforts by church and women's civic groups, a day of Thanksgiving was usually sanctioned in October or November, or at other appropriate times of the year- the abatement of an epedemic for instance-throughout colinial times. Those days were usually spent at church or in prayer, with little of the feasting that is associated with the all festival that was celebrated.

After meeting went to Mr. Daggetts, bought two tickets, in company with RS then drank with my friends and had some discourse with Richard(son)concerning a Bang for night in which we seemed some (what) divided, however we settled the affair in my favour-then we returned to Uncle Jonathan'sand eat the fat and drank the sweet, then I went up to Adj. Daggetts and took (a) horse and rode up to (?) where I blest myself in finding LJ (?) with out trouble & saw Doct. Bliss and his Lady then we returned to N. Wd and spent the evening in jollity among many of my friends(.) About 2 o'clock returned to (?)

Saturday 28th November 1778
Arose and Pack'd up and marched from home(the sun about an hour high) to Uncle J(onathn)'s & SV and took R(ial) in to my company and marched on again.
Made several stops through the neighborhood and took on our backs some cloathing to carry to the camps, however we marched on, discovered nothing remarkable, heard nothing strange.
Arrived in camp by Day light down found considerable peacible times and no fault in our being gone but was some provoked in finding a soldier turned in to our room.
Sunday 29th November 1778
Arose and went to making muster rolls in which I spent the day.
Monday 30th
Rainey morning, however I went over to the Capt. quarters & spent the day with RS in making Pay Rolls.
Returned and got supper & the Capt. sent for me again so I went over and saw Sergt. Smith and spent the evening in writing.
My brother returned from home & tarried with us…
Tuesday 1st December 1778
Arose and got Breakfast and went over to the Capt's to writing & finishing of rolls &c. in which I spent the forenoon.

Afternoon returned & spent the day in reading.

Wednesday 2nd

Got Breakfast and went up to Roll Call. Was informed by Sergt. Smith Capt. Cole had appointed me Sergt. in his company and was called as Sergt.

Drew some provisions...

Thursday Dec 3rd 1778

Attended Roll Call then took a walk out of camp with Sergt. Smith. Stopt at Chaces Tavern and drank; then walked on about three miles from camp to a gold smith's[207], then returned to Chases and drank Sangarea (Sangria) and got Dinner. Then returned home the sun about one hour high. Walked over to Mr. Slades and bought some meal, returned home and had suppawn for supper then had considerable discourse with Mr. Wilber by way of argument.

Friday 4th December 1778

Very Pleasant morning.

In the forenoon nothing strange passed,

Afternoon went down to JW and got my shoes mended.

Saturday 5th

After breakfast went over to the Capt's quarters, then to DW and down to the shore and divided some wood.

Returned and got some(what) wet with rain, then went after fowl at the shore and got wet.

After dinner went to the Capt.'s quarters in answer to his request.

Returned and played checkers with a man deaf & dum...

In the evening reckoned in the mess...

---

[207] Likely Benjamin Burt Jr., who followed his father into the family business in Little Compton. He was also the brother of John Burt who graduated from college in 1756 and became an ordained minister in Bristol, Rhode Island. Sickly when the British attacked the town in May 1778, he had dropped dead in a field attempting to escape the bombardment. (Eliot, John *A Biographical Dictionary: Containing A Brief Account of the First Settlers and Other Eminent Characters Among the Magistrates, Ministers, Literary and Worthy Men of New England* Boston, Cushing & Appleton 1809 p. 108)

Sunday 6th December 1778

Arose and found a very pleasant morning so Rial and I was appointed cook, so he got a quart of milk and made a pot of milk porrage which caused us some laughter as he made them fifteen (?) above proof by making them almost as thick as suppawn; however made out a very good Breakfast then I spent some hours in writing for ye Capt.-

Had an excellent dish of Bak'd beef[208] for dinner-then passed some time in writing.

Towards night went out to the Capt.'s quarters after the Capt. giving us a dram through ye company, we marched after sunset to Slades Ferry and passed muster by candlelight…returned and went with Capt. Stanley over to the Capt's quarters and draw bread, then come back and supped, then had several ladies to set with us who favored us with singing several pleasant songs; wherefore the evening passed agreeable to all ye company.

Then we took a walk and waited on the ladies home & returned and about nine o'clock turned in for sleep.

Monday 7th December 1778

Arose and got Breakfast and spent the forenoon in writing. Afternoon played checkers with Mr. Wilber for a reckoned[209]… spent the evening in the same manner.

Tuesday 8th

Spent the major part of the day in writing-which was attended with considerable rain, which was the state of last night. Spent the evening at Sergt. Smith's.

The Day is past, so run our glass
To shorten our days
 And stop our play…[210]

---

[208] What we would call "pot roast" today.

[209] A wager or bet.

Wednesday, 9th Dec. 1778
Arose and got Breakfast and spent some time in writing of orders, then washed some of my cloathes
Towards night my brother came to set with me who had been to Providence with boats from, thence home who brought me the agreeable news of my Father's health and friends also, a letter from J. Daggett agreeable intelligence...
In the evening E. Loring was at our quarters, thus the evening passed in divers enjoyment

Thursday 10th December 1778
y Brother & W(illia)m B(aco)n got Breakfast with us & set off for their quarters.
In the forenoon spent some time in writing orders. Then I went down to shore, to see what was become of our wood, which I found to be floated off by the tide or stolen.
Returned & helpt load some wood for Mr. Wilber.
Afternoon very rainey so I kept to my quarters and did some writing.
In the evening played checkers with Mr. Wilber.
Friday 11th December 1778
Last night very stormy and some snow on the ground.
This morning was very short for bread as well as for some days-last kivering[211] by borrowing and buying bread and meal &c....

---

[210] A proverb, if you will of religious origin, certainly a variation on a popular theme in Christianity. Compare to these words from a sermon preached a hundred years before by Minister Anthony Farindon of London...*Our time is set, it may be so many years, it may be so many months, it may be so many days, and if we return before our glass is run, there can remain nothing but an expectation of a flood and wrath to be poured down upon our heads...*" (Farindon, Anthony, *Forty Sermons Preached at the Parish-Church of St. Mary Magdelane, Milk Street, London* Printed by F.G. for Richard Marriots, and to be sold at his Shop under St. Dunstan's Church in Fleet-street, 1663).

[211] Covering- "kiver" being a term of Old English still common in New

In the forenoon went to Capt. Cole's quarters to writing, returned at noon and dined on Roast Beef and dumplings. Afternoon, played checkers with Mr. Wilber and spent some time in reading History.

Spent the evening in play.

Saturday 12th December 1778

This morning very pleasant, however we had not any bread so we set (off) to Mr. Slades and bought (a) peck of meal and made suppawn[212].

Spent the forenoon in writing and walking round the camp getting my shoes mended.

Afternoon was at Capt. Cole's quarters then down to the shore and shoved off a boat.

Returned and assisted the Capt.in delivering out cartridges to the men...drew some bread & had potatoes and meal and under comfortable circumstance.

Sunday 13th December 1778

This morning very stormy, so I got Breakfast and went to the Capt. to writing in which I spent the day, dined with Sergt. Smith.

England at the time of Robinson's journal. (de Vere, Maximillian Shele, *Americanisms: The English of the New World* New York, Charles Scribner 1872 p. 497)

[212] Provisions for troops and inhabitants alike were scarce that winter-crops had been destroyed by the same storm that had lashed the troops in Tiverton and Bristol as they waited to invade Aquidneck that summer. By the following January, shortages had become so severe that Rhode Island governor William Greene would write to both Congress and Governor Clinton in New York that "...the necessary article of bread is so scarce in this state, that the General Assembly have directed me to write...requesting that the embargo may be so far dispensed with, as to permit flour and grain to be transported by land from your state, for the sole purpose of feeding the inhabitants of this". He went on to explain that with the British occupying "near one third of the best plow-land in this state", and "large bodies of militia we have been obliged to keep on duty the whole time, we have not been able to improve the lands that we have remaining in our possession". (Bartlett, John Russell *Records of the State of Rhode Island and Providence Plantations* Providence, Cooke, Jackson & Co. 1863 Vol. 2, p. 499)

The day continued stormy, however we had grogg to drink. At night returned to my quarters and read the news print (sup'ed and turned in...nothing remarkable for news...[213]

Monday 14th December 1778

Arose and found fair weather, got Breakfast and went over to Mr. Slades &c.

After dinner was at Capt. quarters and assisted him in paying of the soldiers money. Thus I spent the day. In the evening played checkers with Mr. Wilber.

Tuesday 15th December 1778

Fair and Cold morning, so I got Breakfast and went over to Capt. Cole's quarters and received money for my present service to the amount of Fifty pounds, fourteen Sh(illings), eight pence.

Returned and got dinner & spent some time in writing In the evening O(liver)B(lac)k(inton) returned from Attleboro with a letter from Joseph Daggett to me with the agreeable news of health...

Wednesday 16th

Arose and went down to the Capt's quarters and did some writing. Also got leave for S. R(ichar)d(so)n to go home so I returned and sent a letter home by him, then returned to the Capt. to writing in which I spent the remainder of the day. Spent the evening at home in play

A Pleasant Day
to run away

Thursday 17th December 1778

This morning windy & lousy..reckoned and paid of Mr. Willbour for milk, meat, potatoes, fowls, &c...

---

[213] Although the war had disrupted printing of many newspapers, a few remained for readers in Massachusetts. Robinson likely read a Boston newspaper, either the *Boston Gazette*, or the *Continental Journal and Weekly Advertiser* or perhaps the newly published *Evening Post*. (Wikipedia, *List of Massachusetts Newspapers*)

After Breakfast went to the Capt's quarters to writing, however we spent considerable time in Vendewing & wath and drinking grogg &ccc.

Towards night returned home. The after part of the day being very stormy, I got wet. Nothing further singular...

Friday 18th

Pleasant morning.

Got Breakfast and went over to the Capt's quarters, from thence down to the shore in order to cross the river[214], but the boat being leakey, we returned and went by Slades Ferry to Col. Jacobs quarters and did some writing got the Ensign &ccc.

Returned home and dined then went down to the shore after fowl. Killed one but the wind and tide carried it adrift, that I would not get him. So I returned very much complent.

In the evening went to Mr. Slades to lottery drawing however I proved unfortunate in the seeane, then home from thence to the Capt's quarters and wrote him a letter...then home.

Saturday 19th Dec. 1778

Arose and went before Breakfast to the Capt. quar(ters) and he going out of camp, I drest his hair and received orders that to imploy myself about...then returned home and got Breakfast and went to the Capt. quarters to making a State Pay-Roll in which I spent the major part of the day.

Returned home at night and saw Mr. W(ill)m(ar)th and S.R. who came from Attleboro.

No news of Late.

Sunday 20th Dec. 1778

---

[214] This supports the theory that the encampment was southeast of Slades Ferry, and that the closest access to the shore was likely in the vicinity of a dock described on an 1812 map of the city as "Durfee Wharf". (Map of Fall River, 1812, Wickipedia Commons)

Pleasant morning, however before noon the weather turned lousy-about 11 oc'clock set out (with) Mr. Willmarth to Quaker meeting about a miles walk. So we heard the discourse which was carried on by womankind, and was nothong very awakening in my opinion.....[215]

Returned home and dined and had some discourse with Mr. Willmarth. In the evening Sergt. Smith and a number of Ladies was to see Mr. Willbones and the (evening) passed in singing...

Monday 21st December 1778

The morning warm and pleasant, so I got Breakfast and went to the Capt's quarters and spent the forenoon in making out a Pay-Roll.

Returned and found my brother at our quarters then went to the shore after fowl. Returned, and my brother and Wm Bt dined with us then took a walk up to Mr. Slades. I saw some (?) and Ladies returned and on my return lost a handkerchief. My brother returned and tarried the night & later left our quarters.

---

[215] The Swansea Friends Meeting House built in 1702 had undergone several renovations by the time of Robinson's visit. The original building was only 24 feet wide, but enlarged in 1746 to include side bays and a second floor, which housed a large, open room. The adjacent cemetery is believed to date back to the same early period, with a number of unmarked graves preceding the existing gravestones. Robinson likely heard the witness of Patience Greene Brayton (1733-1794), a well-known woman within the Quaker communinty-and, as her memorial behind the meeting house reads, a "wife, mother, minister, abolitionist. She devoted her life to the freedom of all". Her devotion to the ministry took her to meetings throughout New England as well as England, Ireland, and Philadelphia. She married abolitionist Preserved Brayton and raised three children with him. Bouts of ill health kept her ministry confined to meetings in Massachusetts and Rhode Island toward the end of her life. Raised a Congregationalist, Robinson would have found the discourse of a woman in church a novelty, and unsurprisingly, little more to comment upon.(National Parks Service Ref. # 4000156, Lindley, Susan Hill & Stebmer, Eleanor J. editors, *The Westminister Handbook To Women in American Religious History* London, Westminster John Knox Press 2008 p. 24)

Tuesday 22nd Dec. 1778
This morning cold and clear and considerable snow on the
ground. My brother tarried and got Breakfast then we went
over to the Capt's quarters to writing in which I spent the
forenoon.
Returned and my brother and W(illia)m B(aco)n dined with us
then set off for their quarters and I to the Capt's to my Pay-
Rolls
At night returned home and got supper and spent some time
in (?) then set down and wrote the aforesaid remarks of the
day and night.

Wednesday 23rd Dec. 1778
Last night at going to bed tried the following project (viz)
Took the quarter off my Right Leg, and went out doors &
named three starrs. Winding the quarter round my left thumb
once at each name then un drest and put my quarter under
my head & went to bed backwards with out any discourse
until I had counted twenty backwards & forwards….
I dreamed about one of the names which I gave to the stars.
Got Breakfast and went to the Capt's quarters and had some
parading about the Capt's watch which I bargained for(,)
however it making some difficulty with Sergt. Smith I gave up
the Bargain to Smith and Srink in Peace.
Then spent the day in writing and the evening passed in some
disputes and plays…
Dined with the Capt.

Thursday 24th Dec. 1778
Last night very cold. Got Breakfast and went over to the
Capt's quarters did some writing then traded with Capt. Cole
for a watch which cost me thirty-six pounds.
Then went over to Col. Jacobs quarters at Fall River and got
the ensign and did some other business &c.

Returned home then went to the Capt's and made report. Returned and eat Baked Mutton, and very exceeding cold day passed.

Friday 25th Dec. 1778
Very cold day, however I got Breakfast and went to usual abode for writing in which I spent some time.
This being a day called Christmas; there was to be a cockfight about half a miles distance so I left my writing and went with the Officers to the battles, but it not being very entertaining to me, I returned home.
Dined & then to the Capt's and wrote Sergt Smith a Sergt. Warrant then home play with Mr. W.....
Saturday 26th Dec. 1778
Last night a snow storm which continues very tedious, however I got Breakfast & set out to go to the Capt's but the storm being so tedious I returned and give out going.
However the Capt. soon sent for me so I bundled out and a tedious time I had, however I went to work on making a state Pay-Roll.
Dined with Mr. Shearman at Night. Returned and a very unpleasant walk I had, being almost stifled in the storm[216].

Sunday 27th Dec. 1778
Arose and found the face of the earth covered with snow. However I got Breakfast and went to the Capt's to writing in which I spent the major part of the day.

---

[216] The winter of 1778 would prove to be one of the coldest in the state's history, with the harbors at Bristol and Newport freezing over for weeks at a time. Sentries were in danger of freezing to death at their post. Lafayette, whose Continental encampment crowded Fort Hill, retreated to the home of Simeon Potter in Swansea. (Howe, George *Mount Hope: A New England Chronicle* New York, Viking Press 1959 p. 91)

Dined with ye Captain & Mr. Shearman-toward night returned and in the evening had some singing in Mr. Wilbours Room, then some discourse passed by way of argument.

Monday 28th Dec. 1778
Very Pleasant morning, so I got Breakfast and went to the Capt's quarters and finished off a state Pay-Roll and drank some Grogg &c.
About Two o'clock returned home and dined; having not bread, we borrowed of Mr. Wilbour who promised he would not lend us much longer, saying the state might fund us or we go without.

Tuesday 29th Dec. 1778
About the suns rising Mr. Willmarth came upstairs and said he believed there was an alarm for their firing at the Neck. (I answered) I believed we were dismissed, so I arose and one of the Majors went over to the Capt's and found my imagination true, then we blustered round, some one way and some another returning in cartridges, camp utensils, &ccc.
Settled with Mr. Wilbour and bid good cheer and at half after one (o'clock) we marched for home over banks and valees...
Marched as far as Miles Bridy (and our company being four in number) (viz) G.S.V., E. Willmarth, R. Stanley and myself we drank two mugs of flip then put on feeling very happy...
Some of the company were almost beat out before we go(t) to Morses in Attleboro it being about ten at night. Then drank and warmed and marched on again and arrived at home about 2 o'clock at night mor. and found my Father well.

Wednesday 30th Dec. 1778
Pleasant Continental Thanksgiving day morning so I got Breakfast and a number of my acquaintences came to our house and walked with me to meeting, where I heard Mr. Welds preach.

After meeting went to Daggetts and drank (to) each other's health-then returned home and Mr. J.R. S. went to supper with us, then we went to the s(chool)house and spent the evening in singing tunes then in fiddle dancing-tarried with Rial Stanley.

Thursday 31, Dec. 1778
Arose and got Breakfast with Uncle J(onathan) then returned home and J. Read & R.St(anley) with me-soon after Mr. Wm Barrows and J. Daggett came in who sat the forenoon eith us and went to dinner at the usual time. Meanwhile (,) much jollity past by way of jovial conversation.

About 2 o'clock lasted the detachment…then went down to Uncle B. Stanley's, from thence to Uncle J(onathan) Stanley the to Wm W(ill)m(a)rth-S(tanley) R(obinson) from thence to Mrs Barrows then to Mr. Samuel Stanley's from thence to Mr. Drown; then returned to Mr. Samuel Stanley's from thence to Mr. William Stanley's where we had a fiddler and fiddle gentlemen and Ladies, then the evening passed in jollity… about 9 o'clock returned home and turned in, thus the day and year passed and is gone…

Friday 1ˢᵗ January 1779

Behold the day and year come in with a very pleasant morning so I arose and discharged about half a dozen guns for a happy New Year which were answered from the falls by R. Stanley &c[217].

I spent the day chiefly at home. Towards night Mrs Milley Draper & Naba[218] came in to our house. Then I went to Mr. Pullens with em' from thence to W. Whittikers then returned home…

In the eveningI was at Mr. Pullens and walked out with the Ladies until I met J. Daggett then I returned home and got supper, then walked with W. Daggett up to Daniel S's from thence to Mr. Hds and then to Mr. Orms(?) from thence to Mr. Maxey, and drank with my friends from thence I went up the (?) to (?) wher I found AD[219] in her room alone and (?) thus the night passed…

Saturday 2ⁿᵈ January 1779

Very pleasant morning, so I descended the pasture and on my return met Mrs. Milley Draper[220] who informed by way of news that the ship that her sweetheart was in (or had been) was driven off the last great storm and seventy men frozen.…

---

[217] Attleborough Falls is a triangular area bordered by the Ten-Mile River at the north, Mount Hope street to the west, and Towne street to the southeast. At the time of Robinson's writing this was still a rural area of farmland and small industry on the river. (Commonwealth of Massachusetts, *NRHP Nomination for Attleborough Falls Historic District* 2003)

[218] Likely a nickname for Abigail, her younger sisiter.

[219] Likely Abigail Draper, whom he would later marry.

[220] Millie Draper (1758-1824), who lost her sweetheart just before her twenty-first birthday, would later marry silversmith Samuel Draper, and

(the news I hear, is true I fear)
then returned home and did some writing &c.

Spent the remainder of the day visiting my friends

Sunday 3rd January 1779
Walked to meeting with several of my friends and heard Mr.
Welds preach.
Also the news I heard yeaterday was confirmed and that
among the lost Mr. Hart Man.&c.
Returned home & in the evening was at Mr. Pullens and read
the news print.
Finis.
The object of this little book, being now clear of the Army and
the Campaign completed, consequently it would be needless
and difficult for the simple object to continue his foolishness
any further,,,,,
Attleboro 12th February 1779
Experienced knowledge that while I am used well, to be
contented would be great gain.
Not to be led by superfluous fancy would be a great
advantage. To (think) my company is not my equal is folly
and madness and will terminate in sorrow and disgrace.
Caution,
Let not man think his purse and cloathes will give eternal
happiness or continual contentment and promotion
But each one walk in peaceably and contentedly on his
allotment and not be led by Pride and the Devil who are the
destruction of many in this world, and that which is to
come.....
Yours, Noah Robinson

---

bear him three children, Samuel, Josiah, and Herbert. Josiah would
become a prominent silversmith and jeweler on his own right, in the town.

View from present day Fort Hill, where Lafayette's troops encamped, Bristol

Swansea Friends Meeting House, circa 1702 in present day Somerset, Massachusetts.

Later Diary Entries

May 6th 1781
Sunday
This day I arrived from Salem[221] at Thatchers about 9 o'clock where I fell in company with Doct. Brinton & hear J. Reed[222] with whom I went to meeting & heard Mr. Simmons. On my way home saw J. Draper who was then very sick with fever. Returned home & found my Father & friends in Health.
Monday, 7th May
I was at Mr. Mann's and saw many of my acquaintences(,) in the evening I had the happiness of being at (?) where I spent the evening with Miss Draper

---

[221] Bordered largely by the North River to the west, and the sea to the east, the town of Salem was settled in 1626, and holds the distinction of being the first to muster a militia for the defense of multiple communities in 1629, an act, which today, is recognized as the begginings of the Army National Guard. By the time of Robinson's visit Salem was revitalized as a bustling seaport and would continue to grow with merchants' expansion into the China trade in the 19th century. (Bradford Alden, *New England Chronolgy*, Boston, 1843, Hunt, T.F. *Visitors Guide to Salem,* H.P. Ives, 1880)

[222] Joel Read (1753-1826) of Attleborough, married Robinson's cousin Chloe Stanley (B- 1827) and sister of Rial Stanley on August 29, 1779. Read was on the list of the original minutemen for Attleborough, mustered in April 1775 under Capt. Moses Wilmarth. He was also among those who marched on January 5, 1776. he served under command of Col. George Williams on a secret expedition from September 25th through October 29, 1777, and again under with Capt. Samuel Robinson's company of Wade's Regiment in July 1778. e returned to Attleboro after the war and lived on the family homestead. Read would later serve as a state representative for all but two years between 1806 and 1813. In 1818, his name appeared on the list of Officers of the Attleborough Manufacturing Company, whose "city factory" was located on the 7 Mile River. (Daggett, John *A Sketch of the History of Attleborough* pp. 131, 139, 345, 490)

Thursday, August 2, 1787
Rested well last night-Lousy weather this morning. Drank my juice as yesterday
at 9 o'clock wind at southward, sun shin(ing)-went a gunning, no success. dug some root in afternoon, took a ride on the beach, I took a fine sea breeze-

Friday August 3rd. 1787
Rested well last night-
drank some juice as usual, foggy this morning-Eat Breakfast & set off for home-my brother and Samuel Perry came in company as far as Little Rest[223]. Drank Milk Punch & parted. Rode to Allens to dinner- at four o'clock set off for Greeenwich and arrived at Arnold's[224] at 6 o'clock and put up for ye night (,) Drank tea &c.
Bill at (Parkinses?) Little Rest 1/6
Bill at Allens.............................1/8

Saturday 4th
Pleasant Morning.
Bill at Arnold's 3/6
Rode to Warwick to Arnolds to Breakfast, then for home. Arrived there by (?) o'clock found all well.

---

[223] Set in Kingston, Rhode Island, one of it's earliest communities hosted several taverns and inns for travelers, as it was during the colonial period, a "seat" of Rhode Island where the legislature and courts would meet on a quarterly basis. (see McBurney, Christian, *A History of Kingston, Rhode Island* Pettasquamscut Historical Soc. 1982)

[224] The tavern founded by William Arnold was a meeting place for the local militia called the Kentish Guard, which would later form parts of the 1st and 2nd Rhode Island Regiments of the Continental Army. A wooden "bunch of grapes" sign, which signified the tavern on Main Street of East Greenwich, has long been held in the collections of the Rhode Island Historical Society.

Sunday 16 Sept.
Set off for Wrentham[225] to Mr. Brown, tarried ye night.

[225] Established on September 8, 1636, the town had limited settlement until a group of investors purchased the land from Sachem Philip of the Wampanoag in 1662, and set out lots within a 600-acre section, which would become the center of town. By the late 18th century, the borders of the town had shrunk with the branching out and establishment of Foxboro and Franklin in 1778. At the time of Robinson's visit, the most notable event of recent memory would have been the parade of the French general Rochambeau's army which paraded into Wrentham in December, 1782 on their way to Boston from Yorktown, and encamped on the grounds of the present King Philip Regional High Scool.(Wrentham Historical Commission, Wrentham Town Home Page)

The Maxcy-Hatch Tavern, in present-day Somerset, Mass. Photo by the author.

17th Monday

Set off for Mendon[226], rode five or six miles & fell in company with Mr. & Mrs. Fairbanks[227].

Went on to Mr. Fairbanks, drank tea & put up for ye night.

Tuesday 18th 1787

Lousey weather. Rode to Mendon Town in forenoon.

Afternoon Doct. & Mrs Draper came to Mr. Fairbanks.

[226] The original purchase for the settlement of the town, named the Squinshepauke Plantation, was only eight square miles. The town of Mendon was officially incorporated in 1667 and had grown to sixty-four square miles, but whatever homesteads were established were largely burned to the ground in the winter of 1676 during King Philip's War. Mendon would rebuild along the Boston Middle Post Road, present day Mass Rt 16, and by the late 18th century was a thrivring agricultural community. Local lore has it that in 1789, while President Washington was taking his Inauguration Tour, his party stopped at the Ammidon Tavern, a well known Georgian-style Public House on Main Street, but the Innkeepers wife, not recognizing the famous general, politely suggested that they move on to the Taft Tavern in neighboring Uxbridge. There the President was well treated and entertained by the ancestors of William Howard Taft. (Metcalf, John G. Dr..*Annals of the Town of Mendon 1656-1880* Providence, E.L. Freeman 1880, also *Walking Tour of Mendon,* Blackstone Daily, February 9, 1997 See also http://blackstonedaily.com/mendon.pdf)

[227] Likely Laban Fairbanks (1755-1799), and his wife Mary Wheelock Fairbanks. Laban Fairbanks served in the War as well, having enlisted in Mendon on May 18, 1777 as a private in Capt. Isaac Warren's Company of Col. John Bailey's 2nd Regiment of Massachusetts. He was transferred to Valley Forge March 19, 1778 to serve in the Commander-in-Chief's Guard under command of Capt. Caleb Gibbs, and in that capacity saw action at the Batttle of Monmouth, New Jersey, on June 28, 1778. He was discharged on May 19, 1780. At the time of Robinson's journey, the couple would have been married a little more than two years, having one daughter already, and would bear him six more children before his death on March 29, 1799 at his home in Mendon. (Godfrey, Carlos Emmor,*The Commander-in Chief's Guard Revolutionary War* Washington, 1904 p. 162

Wednesday 18th 1787

Lousy weather, at 10 o'clock Rainy & continued all day.

Thursday 20th 1787

Lousy windy weather.

At 10 o'clock Rode to Mendon Town dined at Mr. Torreys.

Had my horses shoe set.

Spent the afternoon at Doct. Drapers & tarried ye night.

Friday Sept. 21st 1787

Pleasant morning. Set off from Mendon over hills & Rocks to Grafton, Oated (my horse) and put on to Worcester[228], a very pleasant place. Dined on Beef & Lamb Pyes and Medallions…at 3 o'clock set off & came to Capt. Samuel Watsons[229] in Lester (Leicester) & put up for ye Night.

---

[228] The area called *Quinsigamond* by the Nipmuc people would become established as an Indian Praying town by Minister Daniel Gookin, who obtained eight square acres from the tribe on July 13, 1674. Less than a year later, with the outbreak of King Philips War, the settlement was abandoned and what buildings had been erected, were burned to the ground. A second settlement was abandoned as well in 1702 with the onset of Queen Anne's War. The town was resettled in 1713 and formally named Worcester after its sister city in Great Britain. The town received an economic boost in 1731 when it was named a "seat" of the newly formed Worcester County. During the time of the Revolutionary War, Worcester was actively involved in the rebellion, famously stockpiling weapons and ammunition smuggled from Boston, and giving shelter to Isaiah Thomas, publisher of the *Massachusetts Spy*, a patriotic newspaper that he would keep in print throughout the war. He also had the distinctive honor of reading the town's copy of the Declaration of Independence from the porch roof of the Old South Church, a site presently occupied by City Hall.(*Hassanamisco Indian Museum History* HIM, 2013, *Proceedings of the Worcester Antiquarian Society* Worcester Historical Society 1899 Vol. 16 pp. 85-100)

[229] Capt. Samuel Watson (1749-1818) first served as Sergeant of the Leicester Militia on the alarm for Lexington. He would later be promoted to Captain and in 1810, be court-martialed for his alleged reluctance to muster his company as ordered. (see *Trials by Court Martial of Capt. Samuel Watson, 2d David Livermore, Daniel Kent, and William Prouty of the 1st Regiment, 1st Brigade, and 7th Division of the Massachusetts Militia 1810* Worcester, Henry Rogers, 1811)

Saturday Sept. 22, 1787
Lousy morning- afternoon set off from Cat. Watsons to Capt.
Drapers in (Sheniar) took lodging for ye Night.

Sunday Sept. 23rd 1787
Pleasant morning, set off (for) meeting but found my self
unable to ride by reason of a pain in my side. Returned to
Capt. Drapers..in the afternoon went to Mr. A. Drapers too
lodging at Capt. Drapers.
Monday Sept. 24, 1787
Feel pretty well except a pain in my rite side which is small-
lousy weather
Kept to close quarters for ye day.
Tuesday Sept. 25th 1787
Pleasant morning- find my self comfortable this morning. at 8
o'clock left Capt. Drapers for home where we had been well
treated- Rode to Mr. Hinkley's at Lester(,) drank a glass of
wine & put on to Worcester.
Dined at Mowers & had good entertainment put on to Grafton[230]
& put up at Bicknall's (?) very thick & noisy. Saw men &
women traveling from ye four quarters of the world.
Wednesday 26th Sept. 1787
Verry pleasant morning, feel verry well & Eat a hearty
Breakfast- put on to Mendon to Doct. Drapers. Dined heartily
on broiled chickens(,) in the Evening had some pain in my
side.

Thurrsday Sept. 27th 1787

---

[230] Evidence would suggest that Robinson likely traveled on horseback
along what is presently known as MA Route 140, a one hundred and seven
mile roadway that stretches on a northeast trajectory from the intersection
of the Old Army Highway (rt. 6) at New Bedford to the intersection of Rt. 12
in Wichendon, a few miles south of the border with New Hampshire.

Rested well last Night- Eat Breakfast and set off for
Wrentham. Lousy windy weather, arrived at Mr. Browns at (?)
o'clock. Eat dinner & feel pretty well. Kept close quarters for
ye remainder of ye day.
Friday Sept. 28th 1787
Swe(a)t some last night however feel pretty well this morning-
pleasant weather.
Rode out with Mr. Brown in the forenoon-in the afternoon set
off for Attleboro and put up at my Fathers-feel very well this
afternoon.
Sept. 29th
Lousy morning- feel pretty well.
Sunday Sept. 30th 1787
In the forenoon went to Meeting & heard Mr. Avery.
After noon tarried at home.
Monday October 1st 1787
    Rode to Mr. Joel Reed after some Roots. My Father
imployed himself for the Day in gathering Roots and herbs for
a syrup according to the (prescription) given from the old
woman in Grafton[231].
Tuesday Oct. 2nd 1787
Rode in to Providence found my affairs in good order and
friends well.
Returned home by sun set & found my syrup made-[232]
Wednesday Oct 3rd 1787
Rode up to Father Drapers with my Wife & Daughter.
Afternoon went to Col. Mays & spent the Day.

---

[231] From a torn piece of paper that Robinson inserted into his diary:

Roots(:) Sassparella(,) White Soloman Seal, P(an)srey (Pansy?)-made into
syrup in spring water turning from ye North.

[232] Indications are that Robinson was suffering from lung disease or
perhaps was in the early stages of consumption. The herbs listed in the
recipe for the "syrup" were all remedies for respiratory conditions, with the
added prescription that the syrup be made from waters flowing from the
north, or presumably colder, healthier water.

Thursday Oct. 4th 1787
Rode up to Mr. Jn. Drapers & Dined(,) returned to Father Drapers at night.
Friday Oct. 5th 1787
Afternoon went to Doct.Manns & Mr. Stephen Drapers & drank tea.
Returned to my Fathers at Night for Lodging......
Saturday Oct. 6th 1787
Pleasant morning- Returned to Father Drapers-felt weak this forenoon for a while.
Sunday Oct. 7th 1787
Sunday pleasant morning...find my self comfortable-in the forenoon went to Meeting and heard Mr. Strong preach. Returned to my fathers in the afternoon.

Monday October 8th 1787
Rode to Wrentham in the forenoon with Mrs Milley Draper to Mr. Browns-returned to J(osiah) Drapers from thence to Father Drapers[233].
Tuesday Oct. 9th 1787
This day returned to Providence-found all well-put my horse to Olney's[234] at 6p per week.

---

[233] Father Draper being his father-in-law Josiah Draper Sr. (1727-1795) who married Sarah Ellis (1733-1813) their daughter Abigail being the third of eight children. Draper had business dealings in Providence, purchasing"a certain lot of land near King's Chapel on the E side of Benefit Street..." for which he paid The Benevelolent Congregational Society "400 Spanish milled dollars". He later sold the lot "together with all buildings and DWELLING HOUSE with gangway and well privelages" to Abner Daggett, innholder in 1792. (*The Drapers in America*...p, 78, #132, Gowdey, Mary, *Records of #87 Benefit Street* Providence Preservation Society 1964)

[234] Joseph Olney's Tavern lay near the base of the hill of present day Olney Street and the intersection of North Main Street. A large elm on the front lawn of his tavern became Providence's "Liberty Tree", a specimen so large, that a platform was built upon its outstretched limbs to accomadate numerous speakers for the large rally's that gathered there. (Geake, Robert *Historic Taverns of Rhode Island* Charleston, The History Press 2012 p.   )

Wednesday Oct. 10th 1787

Pleasant morning-in the afternoon my Brother set off (for home), who was at Attleboro last Saturday and come into town with me on Tuesday......

Thursday Oct. 11, 1787

Pleasant morning-feel comfortable

Friday Oct. 12th 1787

Pleasant weather-feel pretty comfortable-took a ride for a few miles...

Saturday Oct. 13th 1787

Lousy weather in the forenoon-afternoon pleasant.

Sunday Oct. 14th 1787

Pleasant morning-feel pretty comfortable, set off for Attleboro and arrived at my fathers' abou 2 o'clock.

Monday Oct. 15th 1787

Blustery day. Was at Mrs . I. Drapers,. Jn Drapers, & then to T. Drapers from thence to my fathers who had made me a Second quantity of syrup.

Tuesday Oct. 16th 1787

Very cold(,) windy weather ...

Oct. (?) 1787

Mr. William May came 16th to Board...[235]

Oct. 22nd 1787 Monday

Paul & Aaron Draper came to board[236]

---

[235] The son of the Hon. Elisha May, William May (1764-1790) was then a "student at law at Brown University, from which he would graduate in 1788. He died in the twenty-seventh year of his age. (Hurd, Duane Hamilton, *History of Bristol County, Massachusetts with Biographical Sketches of many of its Pioneers and Prominent Men* Philadelphia, J.W. Lewis & Co. 1883 p. 592)

[236] Paul Draper (1767-1800) was the son of Stephen Draper and Elizabeth Fisher of Dedham, Massachusetts. The family moved to Attleboro and erected a large tannery. Paul was one of five children born before his mother's death. He graduated from Brown University in 1780, and sometime before 1800 'enetered on board an American man of war and was never after heard of..." Aaron Draper (1764-1818) was Robinson's brother-in-law. He graduated from Brown University in 1790, but "never

on the last page in a different hand:

The orange tree in southern Isles
its fragrant branches spreads
Where the poor suffering negro toils
and with his hardships bleeds.

---

studied a learned profession. He eventually settled in Providence where he
lived until his death at the age of fifty-six. (Daggett, *Sketch of the History of
Attleborough* p. 118)

Acknowledgements:

My sincere thanks to Christian McBurney for suggesting this project, and to the staff of the Robinson Research Library of the Rhode Island Historical Society for their assistance with transcribing the diary.
My thanks also must be given to Carl Becker and Norman Desmarais for their thorough reading of the book and advice.

Made in the USA
Columbia, SC
20 March 2018